THE ROYAL
BERKSHIRE
REGIMENT
1914–59

LUDGERSHALL

"As it was in the Beginning"

JUMPING AT DIXON'S

SHERRINGTON CAMP.

NUMBER TWO ORDERLIES!

As it is now

THE ROYAL BERKSHIRE REGIMENT 1914–59

MARTIN MCINTYRE

TEMPUS

Frontispiece: A series of caricatures produced by the 7th (Service) Battalion 1914 whilst in training. They show the new recruit through to the finished soldier. The 7th Battalion was formed in Reading in August 1914 carrying out training on Salisbury Plain. The battalion initially went to France but then went to Salonika where they spent the remainder of the war.

First published 2005

Tempus Publishing Limited
The Mill, Brimscombe Port,
Stroud, Gloucestershire, GL5 2QG
www.tempus-publishing.com

British Library Cataloguing in Publication Data.
A catalogue record for this book is available from the British Library.

ISBN 0 7524 3471 3

Typesetting and origination by Tempus Publishing Limited.
Printed in Great Britain.

Contents

POST OFFICE TELEGRAPHS.

Office Stamp.

If the Receiver of an Inland Telegram doubts its accuracy, he may have it repeated on payment of half the amount originally paid for its transmission, any fraction of 1d. less than ½d. being reckoned as ½d.; and if it be found that there was any inaccuracy, the amount paid for repetition will be refunded. Special conditions are applicable to the repetition of Foreign Telegrams.

Office of Origin and Service Instructions

Charges to pay

s.   d.

Priority Warwick

Handed in at

Received here at

TO: Commanding Depot Barracks

Mobilize group

The Mobilization Telegram from the Warwick manning office to the regimental depot at Reading, which read 'To – Commanding Depot Rdg Barracks, Mobilize group'. It was received at Brock Barracks at 5.40 p.m. on 4 August 1914. Over the following two days the barracks processed 541 reservists, mainly to the 1st Battalion in Aldershot. A further 1,259 reservists were processed on 8 August and sent to the 3rd Battalion at Portsmouth. By 11 November 1918, four years later, the Regiment had amassed fifty-five battle honours, and a total of 313 Officers and 6,375 other ranks had been killed in action, or died of wounds whilst serving in the Regiment.

On receipt of the call-up telegram the reservists report to the guard room, Brock Barracks, Oxford Road, Reading on 4–5 August 1914. These were the first of many. These cloth-capped old soldiers, most of whom had served for seven years with the colours, are signing in whilst being overseen by a fresh-faced recruit on guard duty. On the right a reservist, with hands in pockets, is seen having a chat with (possibly) old comrades, no doubt recounting tales from the African Veldt, or the North West Frontier. These men were quickly equipped, and moved on the 1st Battalion.

Introduction

In essence, this is a photographic book entirely devoted to events in the life of the Royal
Berkshire Regiment. It is not intended to be a history, but rather a selection of pictures
from the regimental archives that have been deposited over many years. Up until now
they have remained unseen by old soldiers and members of the general public alike.

The regiment's early service falls outside the scope of this book, but a number of events
that later led to nicknames and the wearing of certain regimental insignia may require
explanation. To provide a brief history, the Royal Berkshire Regiment existed as a unit in
the British Army Order of Battle from 1743–1959 when, due to army cut-backs, it was
amalgamated with the Wiltshire Regiment (Duke of Edinburgh's) to form the Duke of
Edinburgh's Royal Regiment. The 49th of Foot, later the 1st Battalion Royal Berkshire
Regiment, was raised in Jamaica in 1743 and the 66th of Foot, later the 2nd Battalion
Royal Berkshire Regiment, in 1758.

This volume picks up with the Regiment's entry into the First World War and, like all
regiments at that time; they increased the numbers of frontline battalions substantially.
Most of the Royal Berkshire battalions fought on the Western Front, but the 1st/4th also
served in Italy, and the 7th in Salonika.

After the First World War, the regiment reverted to two regular battalions rotating on
foreign service, with one territorial battalion serving in the county of Berkshire. Between
the wars, the regiment served in Mesopotamia, Persia, Waziristan, Ireland, India, Egypt,
Germany and Palestine.

On the outbreak of the Second World War, events repeated themselves and the
regiment again expanded to meet the challenge, seeing action in France, Italy, Burma
and Germany. At the end of the war, the 2nd Battalion remained in Burma, becoming
the last British regiment to leave that country, after which the 1st and 2nd Battalions
amalgamated in Eritrea in 1949. At that time, they were engaged in anti-Shifta terrorist
operations. The 1st Battalion then served in Egypt, West Germany, Malta and the United
Kingdom, concluding with three gruelling years operating against EOKA terrorists in
Cyprus.

After the Second World War, the territorial battalions merged into the 4th/6th Battalion
and remained so until 1967, when they became part of the Wessex Regiment.

The regimental cap badge worn throughout the period covered by this book was 'The
China Dragon', which the Regiment was permitted to wear after actions by the 49th
Regiment of Foot in the First Opium War 1840–43. The cap badge had a red triangle
backing called 'The Brandywine Flash', which was to commemorate the actions of the
light company of the 49th of Foot at the Battle of Paoli during the American War of
Independence in 1777.

The nickname of the Regiment was 'The Biscuit Boys', which reflected the close proximity of Brock Barracks to the Huntley & Palmer biscuit factory in Reading, a well-known supplier of biscuits to the British Army.

The style and order of presentation of this book has been dictated by the quantity and quality of images available. The photographs have been selected to give as wide a coverage as possible of the regiment's activities both in war and peace. It is, however, restricted at times by the availability of photographs, particularly during active service. Every effort has been made to maintain a balance between the cover given to different battalions of the regiment; this has not been an easy task as, despite the many hundreds of photographs to choose from, some battalions kept comprehensive photographic albums, while those of others have not survived or were less conscientiously maintained. Whilst the 1st/4th Battalion during the First World War, and the 6th and 10th Battalions during the Second World War may appear over-represented, this is only due to a lack of usable material from the others. Some of them have appeared in the Regimental Journal, *The China Dragon*, but the majority have never been previously reproduced and, for conservation reasons, are held in the Regimental archives, unavailable for viewing by the general public.

The captions are subsidiary and are intended to place the pictures in context, providing details of circumstances, dates and, where known, individual identities. As many regimental heroes and characters as possible are portrayed, but it has only been practical to give the briefest of resumes of their careers.

I hope this book conveys throughout a sense of the family spirit of the Royal Berkshire Regiment, both in terms of brothers-in-arms, drawn mainly from the County of Berkshire, and also to the continuity of families serving in the regiment, generation after generation. It is this that has been such a great source of tenacity during battles of the past. Furthermore, it continued after amalgamation into the Duke of Edinburgh's Royal Regiment, and today within the Royal Gloucestershire Berkshire & Wiltshire Regiment.

The great majority of photographs in this volume are held in the Royal Gloucestershire, Berkshire & Wiltshire Regimental archive at the Regimental Museum, The Wardrobe, Salisbury, Wiltshire, and are reproduced with the permission of the Regimental Trustees. Thanks also to the Imperial War Museum, for the following pictures: SE 3441, Q 56796, Q 56803, SE 3332, F 3103, F 3104 and the Oxfordshire County Photographic Archive. Thanks are also due to Les Devine, 'Mac' MacCarthy, Andrew Tatham, Ian Nash, Peter Reader, 'Roz' Robinson, Roger Griffiths, Catherine Hemmings, 'Ned' De Carteret, John Mulford, and the Royal Berkshire Regiment project group (Ian Cull, Len Webb & John Chapman). I am particularly grateful for all the advice and regimental guidance given by the ex-curator John Peters, also the work carried out by museum volunteer Richard Long Fox, whose many hours of hard work and dedication in cataloguing and scanning the photographic archive has made this possible. Last but not least the regimental museum curator Lt-Col (Rtd) David Chilton, whose enthusiasm to make the archives available to the public has been the driving force behind this project.

M. McIntyre
The Royal Gloucestershire, Berkshire & Wiltshire Regiment Museum (Salisbury),
The Wardrobe, 58 The Close, Salisbury, SP1 2EX.
tel. 01722 419419
www.thewardrobe.org.uk

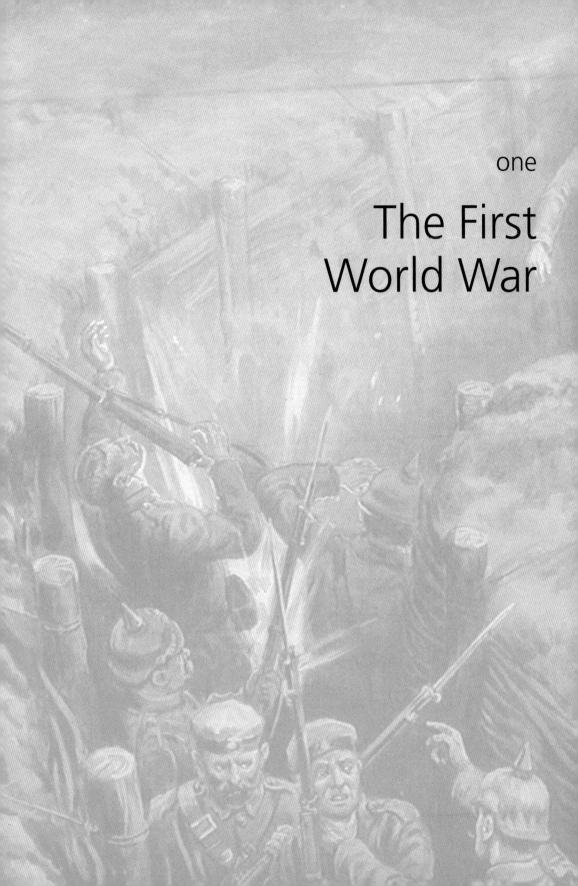

one

The First
World War

The first contingent of reservists being inspected on the square at the depot of the Royal Berkshire Regiment at Brock Barracks, Reading, August, 1914, after which they proceeded to Aldershot to join the 1st Battalion. The officer on the right (with stick) is Major Foley, Officer Commanding the depot who went on to form the 5th (Service) Battalion and was later wounded in France. Most of the men on parade would have had a minimum of seven years' service with the colours. The barrack block behind the men is still in use by today's territorial army.

Having been processed through Brock Barracks, Reading, these newly arrived Reservists wait outside the 30-yard range in Mandora Barracks, Aldershot, after joining the 1st Battalion. The transport officer later remembered, 'These arrived in Batches; Viz 100 on Aug 5th, 400 on 6th, and 100 on 7th they were very unfit. Since going to the reserve their feet had grown and all their boots seemed too small. They could barely march 3 Miles with their kit on. They spent sometime in the canteen where they drank rather a lot.'

The 1st Battalion on the march, led by the band, at Aldershot shortly after mobilisation. They are marching back to Mandora Barracks, after an inspection by Their Majesties King George V and Queen Mary on 11 August 1914. Two days later they landed in France, and by 24 August these men were taking part in the retreat from Mons.

For gootness sake Halt !
der Royal Berks.
are koming.

A First World War postcard adjusted to suit the buyer's regiment. This card was sent by Private Albert Geater of the 1st/4th Battalion Royal Berkshire Regiment to his ex-employer Mr Simmon's, Market Place, Wantage. Pte Geater was killed in action on 16 August 1917. He has no known grave and is commemorated on the Tyne Cot Memorial to the missing.

The Drums and Bugles of the 8th (Service) Battalion, lead the Battalion through the streets of Reading after a route march. This corps of drums was formed only a few weeks before departure for the front. Some of the drummers would have been in their village bands at home and as a consequence had some basic musical knowledge. The youngsters following the drum on either side would be ready to join up by 1918.

New Year's Eve, 1914. Soldiers of the 7th and 8th (Service) Battalions in a festive mood at a party given in their honour by the Broad Street Reading Congregational Church prior to departure to the front. By the following year the 8th Battalion had been 'Blooded' at the Battle of Loos, and the 7th Battalion were in a very different theatre of operations, Salonika.

Soldiers of the 7th and 8th (Service) Battalions steam out of Reading railway station en route to other training camps to continue their training. They were seen off by the Mayor of Reading and the local newspaper recorded, 'in response to much hand waving by the watching crowd the sounds of "Tipperary" drifted back'.

The 4th Territorial Battalion march into their war station of Chelmsford after a seventy-mile march from Dunstable on Monday 24 August 1914. They are headed by the battalion's corps of drums with their drums carried on their back. This was very much a Berkshire battalion with the vast majority of the men coming from the county.

Newly arrived recruits for the 2nd/4th Battalion, September 1914, who assembled at Hitcham
Farm near Marlow, Buckinghamshire. The farm was owned by Colonel H. Hanbury VD, a volunteer
officer of many years standing who raised the battalion. Some of these men are in civilian clothes
and the conditions are rudimentary. They trained hard and were ready for front-line duties in France
by May 1916, when they went to France as part of the 61st Division.

Three young drummers of the 9th (Reserve)
Battalion in Bovington Camp, Dorset, July
1915. The 9th Battalion was a training battalion
and never saw action as a front line unit, but
the many thousands of recruits who passed
through the battalion did. The three young
soldiers pictured here would have joined one
of the front-line battalions after training, but
what the drum major would have to say about
his drummers using the side drum as a seat can
only be guessed at. In 1916, the 9th Battalion
became the 37th Training Reserve Battalion.

A recruiting campaign in Station Road, Reading, January 1915. A poster appealing to the men of Reading to join their own battalion and to fall in and follow was wheeled in the wake of the procession, which contained 500 troops drawn from the 2nd/4th, and 8th Battalions of the Royal Berkshire Regiment, headed by the Caversham and Reading veteran's band. At tea, in the corn exchange afterwards, the Mayor of Reading congratulated the troops on their strong marching and soldier-like bearing.

Officers of the 5th (Service) Battalion 1915, resting on one of the many route marches in Kent whilst the battalion hardened itself for the ordeal to follow in France. Centre is Lieutenant Cecil Argo Gold, who later became the adjutant and was killed in action on 3 July 1916 when the battalion attacked Ovillers-La-Boisselle, on the Somme. To his left is Lieutenant Patrick Gold, his brother. A third brother, Alec, also served in this battalion. Both Patrick and Alec survived the war. These brothers came from Maidenhead.

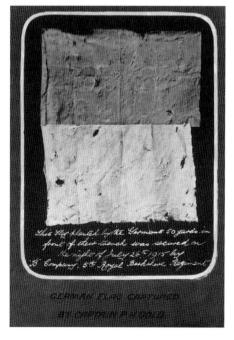

A German trench flag planted by the Germans fifty yards in front of B Company, 5th Battalion's trenches at Ploegsteert Wood. General Wing, on an inspection of the trenches, indicated it might make a fine trophy. This trophy was secured by a patrol under the command of Lieutenant Patrick Gold on the night of 26 July 1915, and later displayed in Maidenhead town hall. After much discussion the tactic for retrieving the trophy was decided by a Sergeant, who said, 'The only thing, Sir is to tie the ***** rope round the ***** flag and pull the ***** thing in.'

Recruits of the 8th (Service) Battalion, outside a barrack hut at Sutton Veney, Wiltshire, where the battalion were in training, displaying a home-made flag which shows the regiment's cap badge, the China Dragon. The old soldiers of the regiment bought in to train these men would have been quick to inject into them the regiment's traditions.

Drummers of the 7th (Service) Battalion lead the battalion back to camp after a field exercise in Wiltshire, 1915. They were based at Sandhill camp, No. 14, at Longbridge Deverill, near Warminster. Note that the drummers and buglers have their rifles slung on their backs. At this time the battalion was under command of Lt-Col Bray, who had fought and survived the Battle of Maiwand with the 66th of Foot in 1880.

Signallers of the 7th (Service) Battalion, on exercise in Wiltshire, *c.*1915. They had to reach a certain proficiency with the signalling flags that they are carrying. Later the reality of battlefield snipers meant they were restricted to either acting as runners or mending broken telephone cables. After training, the battalion initially went to France, but were quickly dispatched to Salonika.

A sight only seen by marching columns of troops. Officer's wives and daughters of the 7th (Service) Battalion, cameras in hand, await the return of the battalion from a training exercise. The photograph is from Lt-Col Bray's album and is believed to have been taken by his daughter. It reads 'Awaiting the "Warriors" return from a field day at Longbridge, September 1915'.

DARING DEEDS.

Acting-Sergt. W. Winter (Distinguished Conduct Medal),
1st Royal Berkshire Regt.

For conspicuous gallantry on November 2nd, when he left
his trench at great risk and recovered a machine gun which
had been buried by a shell. He then worked the gun by
himself, the officer and man previously manning it having
been wounded.

An early First World War postcard depicting 'Daring Deeds', in this case Sergeant Winter of the 1st Battalion. Sgt Winter from Newbury is depicted winning his Distinguished Conduct Medal, the citation reading, 'For conspicuous gallantry on the 2nd November, when he left his trench at great risk and recovered a machine gun which had been buried by a shell. He then worked the gun by himself, the officer and man previously manning it having been wounded'. During this action he was wounded in the eye. These postcards were discontinued towards the end of 1914 when the manufacturers realized that the war would not be over by Christmas, in addition to being overwhelmed by the numbers of actions leading to awards of these Medals. Sgt Winter survived the war and became a taxi driver in Newbury.

Regular soldiers of the Royal Berkshire Regiment in the trenches, 1915. The officer seated to the right is Capt. Alan John Bowles, who served initially in the 1st Batallion and later in the 2nd Battalion where he was killed in action on 10 April 1916. He is buried at Becourt Military Cemetery. The soldier facing (centre) is carrying an extra bandolier of fifty rounds of ammunition in addition to what he would have been carrying in his webbing. This appears to be part of a quiet sector; otherwise the soldier looking over the parapet would soon come to the attention of a German sniper.

The sergeants of the Berkshire National Reserve at Newbury Racecourse, engaged on the duty of guarding prisoners of war and interned aliens. The Newbury concentration camp closed at the end of 1914 when the inmates were transferred to the Cunard Line ships *Ascania* and *Andania* at Spithead; The Berkshire reserve guards went with them. In addition, these men, all old soldiers, were responsible for guarding vulnerable points such as railway bridges. The commanding officer, Major Langford, is sitting in the centre. This unit is badged and administered by the Royal Berkshire Regiment. The significance of the goat is not clear.

Members of the Royal Berkshire Regiment National Reserve escort German prisoners through East London near Stratford railway station en route back to Germany, having been exchanged. Most of these German prisoners were medical orderlies.

Right: The 1st/4th Battalion took over its first front line sector on 15 April 1915 at Le Gheer, on the east face of Ploegsteert Wood. A sentry of the battalion demonstrates the use of a trench periscope in a well-constructed trench system. Although this equipment had limited vision it reduced the number of casualties caused by soldiers inadvisedly looking over the parapet. As a sentry he has his rifle with bayonet fixed close to hand.

Below: The 1st/4th Battalion, in the breastworks to the rear of the front line on the edge of Ploegsteert Wood, spring 1915. This area was very much a familiarisation sector for battalions new to the front to enable them to work themselves up to a state where they could take their place in areas with more activity. Breastworks of this type were normally constructed when it was too wet too dig down.

A sniper pair of the 1st/4th Battalion demonstrate their trade in the roof space of Antons Farm, Ploegsteert Wood, early 1915. The observer with the binoculars would act as an extra pair of eyes for the sniper, and also assist in feeding back to the sniper his fall of shot. As Berkshire was very much a rural county at that time, finding good shots from many of the farm workers in the battalion was not a problem.

After leaving Ploegsteert Wood the 1st/4th Battalion went into reserve and ended up at Hebuterne, in July 1915, having relieved the French. Before entry to the trenches they stayed at Bayencourt, described by the regimental history as 'a stinking little village full of flies and harlots'. Here we see two soldiers of the battalion pumping out the trenches at Hebuterne, late 1915. The conditions here were a little more uncomfortable than those experienced in Ploegsteert Wood.

Sgt Frederick Charles Giles, 1st/4th Battalion, seen here in early 1915 in the trenches at Hebuterne. Sgt Giles was an excellent shot and was particularly active in the area of Pozieres in July 1916, where he accounted for a number of 'Huns' as described by the regimental history. He went on to win the Military Medal and was killed in action on 16 April 1917. He has no known grave but is commemorated on the Thepval Memorial to the missing. He is shown wearing the cloth shoulder title 'Royal Berks' with the number 4 underneath.

A sentry of the 1st/4th Battalion in Batteuse trench, Hebuterne, August 1915. The soldier's rifle has its bayonet fixed ready for instant action. He is fully equipped with the 1908 pattern equipment, each pouch carrying his ammunition. The regimental cloth shoulder title is still worn, although this practice ceased as the war progressed. These trenches were situated on a forward slope looking down on the Germans who were anything from 400 to 900 yards away.

Machine gunners of the 1st/4th Battalion in a posed picture behind the lines at Hebuterne, 1915. The machine gun is a .303 Vickers machine gun which, when in the hands of well-trained soldiers, proved a devastating tool during the First World War. A similar water-cooled machine gun, manufactured by Spandau, was used by the German army. Later in the war, Vickers machine gun teams were grouped together in Machine Gun Battalions of the newly created Machine Gun Corps.

Soldiers of the 1st/4th Battalion resting in the trenches whilst engaged in digging and strengthening their trench position, believed to be Hebuterne, c.1915. Most are wearing cap comforters. Steel helmets were not introduced until the following year. To the left in the dugout is the ever-present rum jar.

Royal Berk's Cemetery, Ploegsteert Wood. This cemetery was started by the 1st/4th Battalion, in 1915 with the burial of Lt Poulton Palmer, the first officer of the battalion to fall. Today it is called Hyde Park Corner (Royal Berks extension) Cemetery and contains the memorial to 11,000 missing soldiers of all regiments.

Number 3 Platoon, A Company, 1st Battalion, pictured behind the lines in 1915, some wearing the 'spoils of war'. Seated first left is the platoon Sgt Edward Jones, a pre-war regular with the 2nd Battalion. He was wounded at Neuve Chapelle, and later, after joining the 1st Battalion, won the Distinguished Conduct Medal, Military Medal and Bar. He died of wounds received on 8 October 1918. He is buried at Delsaux Farm Cemetery at Beugny.

The officers' mess of the 1st Battalion, Bethune, July 1915. This photograph was taken shortly before the Battle of Loos which started on 25 September 1915. The officers maintained a mess throughout the First World War and it was managed by Sgt Astley. (Centre) Capt. M. Radford DSO (KIA 28.9.15), (Left) Capt. Fullbrook-Leggatt, Lt Getting (KIA 28.9.15), RAMC Officer, Capt Boshell DSO, Lt Hall (KIA 28.9.15), Lt Jerwood MC, (Right) Capt. Frizzell DSO, Lt Eagar, Royal Artillery Officer, Lt Gregson-Ellis MC, Lt Stokes MC, Lt Turner VC (DoW 1.10.15).

Officers of the 6th (Service) Battalion, January 1917. From left to right, back row; 2nd Lt Joseph, Lt Wrinham, Lt Kemble, Lt Battans, Revd Parkinson, Lt Tindall (KIA 31.7.17), 2nd Lt Barrett (wounded), Capt. Richardson MC, 2nd Lt Kingham (KIA 10.8.17), 2nd Lt Spencer, 2nd Lt Jackson (wounded), 2nd Lt Bradley. From left to right, front row; Capt. Hudson (Later CO 8th Battalion), Capt. Longhurst (KIA 12.12.17), Maj. Goldsmith, Lt-Col Clay DSO (CO), Capt. Rochfort MC (wounded), Lt Guthrie (QM), Capt. Ackroyd (MO) VC MC (KIA 11.8.17).

An illustration showing Lt Alexander Buller Turner from Thatcham, Berkshire, winning his Victoria Cross on 28 September 1915 during the 1st Battalion Royal Berkshire's assault at Fosse 8 during the Battle of Loos. He is shown bombing his way along a trench system known as Slag Alley. It was in this action that he was wounded, and later died at a dressing station on 1 October 1915. He is buried at Chocques Miltary Cemetery, France.

A platoon of the 6th (Service) Battalion, on the Western Front, 1917. The soldier sat above the cross is Private Harrison who posted this postcard on 27 July 1917 to his mother at Mount Pleasant, Reading. He wrote 'Just a line to let you know I am still alive and kicking. According to this photo I am getting as fat as a "Berkshire Pig", don't you think so', signed Ernie. The postcard would have arrived in Reading, on or about 30 July. On 31 July 1917, Private Harrison was killed in action during an attack at Glencorse Wood. The 6th Battalion lost sixty-seven men in the attack. Pte Harrison has no known grave and is commemorated on the memorial to the missing at the Menin Gate.

On 15 December 1917, a commemoration service for the first seven divisions who helped stem the German Army's advance in 1914, which included the 1st Battalion Royal Berkshire Regiment who served in the 6th Brigade of the 2nd Division, was held at the Albert Hall in London. This banner was produced by the Royal School of Art needlework on behalf of the regiment. It was of royal blue silk, showing the regimental badge. 5,000 postcards were produced, with a lot of the proceeds going to the Prisoner of War fund.

Private Charles Howard Humphreys (right) of the Royal Berkshire Regiment captured in April 1917. He is seen here together with two other prisoners, wearing a prison jacket with armband, prison trousers with a stripe down the side, all to assist in identification in the event of escape. He is still wearing his regimental cap badge. The unidentified soldier (centre) is a Royal Berkshire corporal with one wound stripe on his left arm. This soldier has lost his cap badge, and in order to maintain regimental identity he has utilised his shoulder title 'Royal Berks' as an ad-hoc cap badge.

The only known photograph to exist showing the 1st Battalion moving into the line on 21 August 1918 at Ayette. All the men are fully equipped with bayonets fixed. The war diary entry for the day explains the poor quality of the photo; it reads 'The morning was very misty and it was difficult to keep direction. The tanks especially were soon in trouble and were of little assistance to the Battalion, however all objectives were captured'. Over the following three days the battalion had two officers and twenty-four other ranks killed in action with 200 wounded.

If der Berkshire Regt.
haf gone by, den I kan kom out.

Left: One of many postcards produced during the First World War which were tailored to fit the sender's regiment.

Below: Battlefield clearance, 1919. Soldiers of the 5th (Service) Battalion work together with civilian contractors to clear the battlefield after the First World War. As always infantry regiments were a prime source of manpower for these tasks. Centre, looking towards the camera is the battalion's commanding officer Lieutenant Colonel Goodland, who later brought the battalion cadre back to Reading.

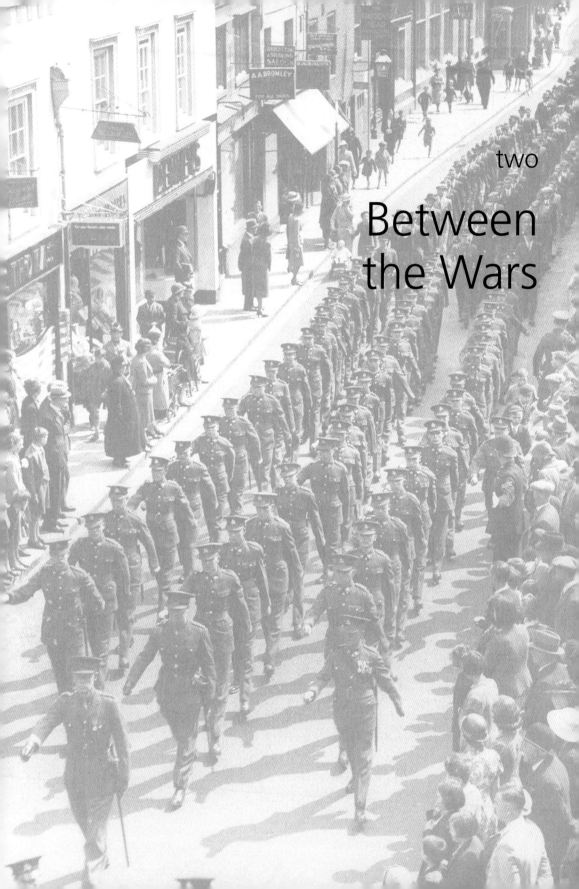

two

Between
the Wars

A postcard purchased by generations of soldiers at embarkation points, prior to going to India for a tour of duty. The postcard displayed the regimental cap badge adjusted to reflect whatever regiment was going, in this case the 1st Battalion Royal Berkshire Regiment.

1st Battalion, on the march, North West Frontier, c.1921. This gives a clear view of the conditions these soldiers laboured under during this period. They would march for fifty minutes, then rest for ten, a practice used by the British infantry over many years. They would keep this up until the route march was complete.

On 1 March 1924, the 1st Battalion left Bareilly on an eleven-day march to Razmak for active service. This is the machine gun section of the 1st Battalion Royal Berkshire Regiment crossing the Shinki Bridge on 7 March en route to the next camp at Idak.

A welcome relief from marching. The ferry at Kalabach with a contingent of the 1st Battalion on board during the same march in 1924.

Death on the Frontier was a way of life to soldiers who served in India. Here, soldiers of the 1st Battalion, during the Waziristan Campaign of 1924–25, carry a comrade to a gun on which the coffin will be carried. The soldiers carrying the coffin would normally come from the soldier's own section or platoon.

1st Battalion in Waziristan 1924–25. The rear of the photograph reads, 'Our arrival at Reading Piquet after a stiff climb'. The soldiers would garrison these outlying piquets for a number of months. Snipers from local tribes the Mahsuds and Wazirs were a problem the battalion soon learned to deal with. An officer of the regiment, Lt-Col, Davidson-Houston, later recalled, '12th April, Tribesman took advantage of the bad weather and heavily sniped the camp at night; We had a guest night and a concert afterwards'.

Soldiers of the 1st Battalion on the march in India *c*.1920, during one of the obligatory ten- minute rest periods, the sweat tells the story. The helmet flashes with 'Royal Berkshire' thereon are clearly visible on the soldiers' helmets.

Foot Inspection on the Frontier. Soldiers of the 1st Battalion line up for a foot inspection by their officers after a day's march. This essential ritual maintained a level of unit fitness that allowed them to march for many miles with the minimum of men dropping out. Regiments at this time prided themselves on the distances they marched and the small number who dropped out, and the Royal Berkshire's were considered to be 'a good marching regiment'. Visible in the background are the Indian water carriers that accompanied all marching columns in India, the task very often being passed from father to son.

2ⁿᵈ Bn. Royal Berkshire Regᵗ. — Tank Section — Dublin, Nov. 1920.

When the 1st Battalion returned to India, the 2nd Battalion remained as the home service Battalion. Here we see the 'Tank Section' of the 2nd Battalion in Dublin, Ireland, November 1920. The 2nd Battalion was posted to Dublin after the war because of the continuing problems in Ireland. The use of the tank by infantry soldiers is not quite clear, but could well be an early example of 'mechanised infantry'.

The 2nd Battalion were part of the British Army of the Rhine from 1926 to 1928 stationed at Wiesbaden. Training was carried out at Sonnenburg where this guard mounting was carried out. The highlight of the tour in Germany was beating the Cameron Highlanders (18-8) in the final of the BAOR Rugby cup.

Fatigue party, 2nd Battalion, Wiesbaden, Germany, *c.*1926. Infantry battalions are like small towns moving from place to place and all manner of duties have to be carried out to allow the organisation to function. As a consequence, many private soldiers, such as the four shown above, spent a considerable amount of time on 'fatigues'. Many fatigue functions were filled by 'defaulters'.

The fatigues in this case were 'spud bashing', or peeling potatoes, with the 1st Battalion, on the march in around 1927 in India. In India it was somewhat easier in terms of manpower to complete these tasks, as all battalions had a number of employed Indian workers to assist, much to the relief of the private soldiers.

CANADA

NIAGARA FALLS

CHINA

READING

HAWKES BAY

NEW ZEALAND

In the 1920s, the War Office produced a scheme to ally individual British regiments with those of the Dominions. The first affiliation for the Royal Berkshire Regiment was the Hawkes Bay Regiment, of Danneverke, New Zealand, who later incorporated the Royal Berkshire Regimental March 'The Dashing White Sergeant' as their regimental march. They later added the Lincoln and Welland Regiment of Canada in 1928 and the 49th Australian Infantry Regiment in 1931.

1st Battalion, Transport Section, Shorncliffe, 1937. This photograph was taken shortly before the battalion changed from horse to mechanized transport. From left to right; Lieutenant Wilder, L/Cpl Bennett, Pte Plank, Pte Bloomfield, Pte Fletcher, Pte Haynes, L/Cpl Dawson, Pte Sorby, Pte Weaver. Horses, from left to right: Punch and Ginger, Peggy and Donk, Tony and Queenie, Nivelle and Nive, Jack and Pongo.

The 1st Battalion, Bareilly, India, 1923. The battalion march on parade, headed by the band and drums, to celebrate the Battle of Bourlon Wood, 1917. There were some members of the battalion who fought in that battle who were still serving. Family members look on.

The machine gun section, 2nd Battalion on manoeuvres in England *c*.1927. This mode of transport would be very welcome to these infantry soldiers.

Side drummers, 2nd Battalion, Egypt, *c.*1936. From left to right: Dmrs Sheppard, L/Cpl Parmenter, Dmrs Goody, Harris, Musgrave, Collett, Beddows and Spencer. L/Cpl Parmenter was an old soldier who had joined the regiment in 1912, fighting with the 1st Battalion throughout the First World War. He was appointed an effective drummer in 1922, becoming the lead side drummer the same year.

Commanding Officer's Bugler 1935–36 in Egypt. Drummer (Boy) A. Steane, 2nd Battalion. This honour was given to the most talented drummer for the half year. The Royal Berkshire flash on the left side of the helmet is clearly visible (Red on Black).

The Drums of the 2nd Battalion march into Talavara Barracks, Jerusalem, ahead of the battalion in 1936. The guard has turned out and is presenting arms. The ceremonial aspect of this posting in Palestine was very high and the band and corps of drums were very busy.

Whilst the two regular battalions soldiered elsewhere, the Berkshire Territorials practice their skills at annual camp each year. Here C Company, 4th Battalion, are seen 'marching through a gassed area' on annual camp, 1938. The experience with gas attacks in the First World War was very much in the minds of these soldiers as they trained. Thankfully gas was not used during the forthcoming Second World War. This column is led by Captain Verey and CSM Jarrett, followed by Ptes Beckley, Wells and Brown, from the Maidenhead Company.

Left: The 4th Battalion march through Maidenhead, on a church parade, 21 May 1939. Four months later war was declared and the 4th Battalion was sent to France. With the fall of France they fought their way back to the beaches at La Panne, near Dunkirk. Forty-seven men of this battalion came off the beach.

Below: B Company 8th (Home defence) Battalion on parade in St Mary's Butts, Reading, on 30 August 1939, prior to moving to Vauxhall Barracks, Didcot. This unit was part of No.84 group, and was initially responsible for guarding 'vulnerable points' such as wireless stations and railway tunnels. In December 1941 they became the 30th Battalion, Royal Berkshire Regiment.

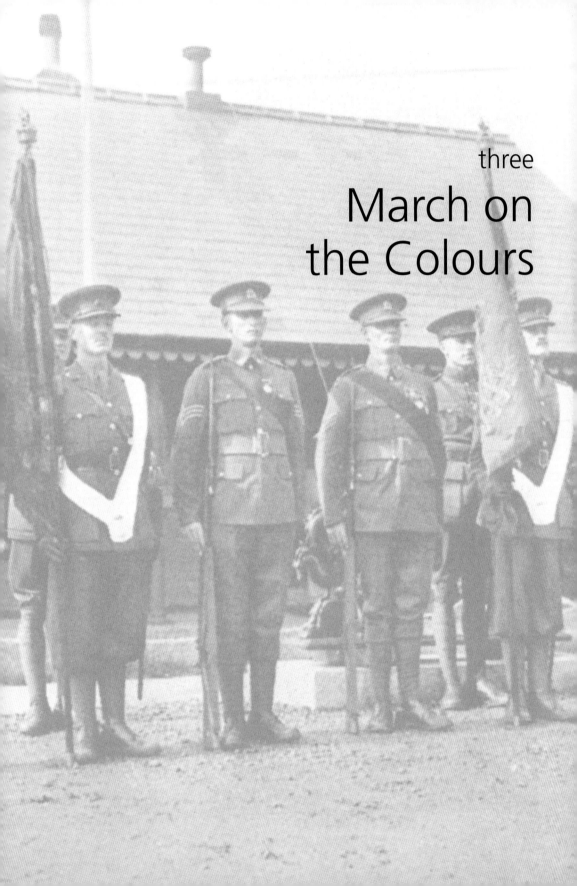

three

March on
the Colours

Presentation of King's Colours to the 6th, 7th, 10th, 11th, 12th and 13th Battalions of the Royal Berkshire Regiment at Brock Barracks, Reading, August 1920, by Major General Sir H.B. Walker KCB, KCMG, DSO. The 6th and 7th Battalions were front-line rifle battalions during the First World War, and the remainder were labour battalions. The regiment was one of very few who presented colours to their labour battalions. Second row with colours, from left to right; Capt. Wood (12th Bn), Lt Hilliard (13th Bn), Brig. Gen. Bodie (11th Bn), Capt Holtham (10th Bn), Major Pike MC (7th Bn), Brig. Gen. Dowell CB CMG (6th Bn). After this presentation, the colours were duly laid up in different Reading churches. All these colours are now missing.

Officers of the 5th (Service) Battalion, with the King's Colour presented to the battalion by the Prince of Wales at Erre, France, on 4 February 1919. Sitting (centre) is the commanding officer, Lt-Col H.T. Goodland, who brought the battalion back to England shortly after this event. After the war Lt-Col Goodland spent many years working for the Imperial War Graves Commission (now the CWGC). This colour was laid up in St Laurence's Church, Friar Street, Reading, where it can be seen today.

A Guard of Honour of the 2nd Battalion, Dublin, 1920. The regimental colour is on parade. This colour was presented by Queen Victoria in 1882 prior to the regiment being designated 'Royal' and, as a consequence, the 2nd Battalion carried the non-Royal white facings on the colour. This colour was carried by the battalion up until the merger with the 1st Battalion in 1949.

The colour party of the 2nd Battalion wheel into position outside St Laurence's Church, Friar Street, Reading, on 6 July 1929. This was when the battalion marched throughout Berkshire to keep the regiment in the public eye. They started the march on 4 July at Wokingham, finishing at Newbury on the 12th, covering most of the county in between.

Colour Party, 1st Battalion, Khartoum 1934, on the forty-ninth anniversary of the Battle of Tofrek. From left to right; Sgt Gammon, Lt Harris, Sgt Downey, Lt Stevens, Sgt Edmonds. The Battle of Tofrek took place in the Sudan in 1885, after which Her Majesty Queen Victoria graciously consented that 'in future The Regiment should be known as The Royal Berkshire Regiment'. This was, and as far as is known, still is, the only occasion where a regiment has been given the Royal title as a result of one particular battle.

The 4th Battalion on the march, c.1930, with 'Cased Colours'. All soldiers are marching with rifles slung at the shoulder, in the 'at ease' position, with the exception of those escorting the (cased) colours who remain at the slope.

The drums and colours of the 2nd Battalion in India prior to the Second World War. From left to right; Boy Soldier Dixon, Drum Major Gilding, Boy Soldier Parsons. The colours, although not carried in battle, are starting to show their age, having been presented by Queen Victoria in 1882, to replace those lost at Maiwand.

The colour parties of the 1st and 4th Battalions, together with the 10th London Regiment (Hackney), at the regimental reunion, Shorncliffe, 1935. The 10th London's was affiliated to the regiment, changing their designation in 1937 to the 5th (Hackney) Battalion Royal Berkshire Regiment. From left to right; Sgt Downey, 2nd Lt Metcalf, Sgt Martin, Sgt Byde, 2nd Lt Howes, Sgt Foster, -?- , 2nd Lt Beer, -?-. To the rear in the centre is RSM Jenkins DCM. He won his DCM in the First World War with the 1st Battalion and served in India in the inter-war years. He retired shortly before the Second World War and, on the outbreak of war, rejoined as the RSM of the 4th Battalion.

The regimental colours being shown to newly enlisted men on the parade square at Brock Barracks Reading, *c.*1940. The idea was to instil in the new recruits the ethos of the regiment they were joining. Great emphasis would have been placed on the battle honours. By the end of the Second World War, many of the men present on this parade would also have been in action when further battle honours were added.

Airport Camp, Asmara, Eritrea, 1949, the colours of the 1st Battalion and the 2nd Battalion, are paraded together for the last time prior to the amalgamation into one battalion as a result of the post-war reductions of infantry battalions.

Right: The colour party of the 1st Battalion, returning its colours to the officers' mess after the amalgamation of the 1st and 2nd Battalions, Asmara, Eritrea, 1949. Rear left as escort to the colours is C–Sgt E. Allen, who later became an RSM. CQMS Merry is in the centre. These colours were carried by the battalion until 1956 when HM The Queen presented new colours at Windsor Castle.

Below: The colours of the 4th/6th Battalion, on display at Annual Camp, Windmill Hill, Lugershall, Wiltshire, 1953. Apart from formal parades this would be one of the rare occasions when soldiers from the battalion would be able to view their own colours.

To show the close links between the town of Wallingford and the local territorial infantry regiment, in 1960, the mayor's mace and the regimental colours of the 4th/6th Battalion were displayed together during a recruiting session in the town. The battle honours are clearly visible. On the left of the regimental colour is a naval crown to commemorate the Battle of Copenhagen of 1801, in which the 49th (later 1st Royal Berkshire) took part as marines under Nelson.

The colour party of the 4th/6th Battalion take the colours into St Mary's Church, The Butts, Reading, on Sunday 11 October 1959 on the occasion of the centenary of the formation of the volunteer movement in 1859, and therefore the Berkshire Rifle Volunteers (later becoming the 4th/6th Battalion). These colours were presented to the 4th Battalion in 1909. The colour party consists of Lts Smallbone and Thompson.

Colour party 4th/6th Battalion Royal Berkshire Regiment, *c*.1963, Brock Barracks, Reading, Queens Colour Lt Thomas (left), Regimental Colour Lt Ravenhill (right) together with RSM Collings and Maj. Frazer. These colours were laid up in 1967 in St Laurence's Church, Reading.

Her Majesty the Queen presenting new colours to the 1st Battalion at Windsor Castle, 21 July 1956. The new colours were received by Lts Tremellen and Redding.

Above: Cased colours of the 1st Battalion being ferried from Malta, *c.*1956, where the battalion was on stand-by for the Suez Crisis and for Cyprus, where they were to spend the next three years engaged in counter-terrorist operations against EOKA. Even when colours are moved around like this, there is always a ceremonial air to the proceedings.

Left: The colours of the 1st Battalion being marched into the State Apartments at Windsor Castle on 22 May 1959. Here they were laid up prior to the regiment's amalgamation with the Wiltshire Regiment. These colours had been presented by HM The Queen only three years before. Lt Jones carries the regimental colour and Lt Morris carries the Queen's colour. Lt Jones later became a commanding officer of the 1st Battalion Duke of Edinburgh's Royal Regiment (Berkshire & Wiltshire) in 1977.

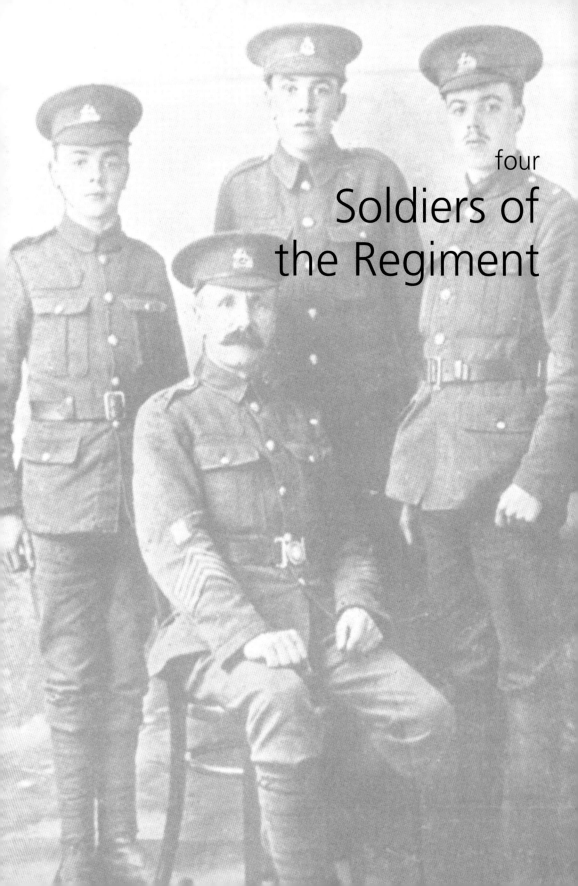

four

Soldiers of
the Regiment

Lt Alfred Burgess DSO, 1st Battalion he was awarded an immediate DSO on 4/5 February 1917, when he led a trench raid that captured two German officers, forty-nine other ranks and killed fourteen. Later the same year he was also mentioned in dispatches. He had previously served in the ranks of the Scots Guards and was commissioned into the regiment. It was very unusual for an officer of this rank to be awarded an immediate Distinguished Service Order. His medals are on display at the Regimental Museum at Salisbury.

Lt William Pat Garnett 3rd Battalion (attached to the Royal Flying Corps), killed in action on 3 March 1917, whilst serving in No. 60 Squadron. He was shot down at Nieuport, and is believed to have been the fourth victory of Lieutenant Kurt Wolff of Jasta 11. After he was shot down, Baron Von Richthofen returned his personal effects to his widow, with an accompanying letter paying tribute to Lt Garnett's flying skills. He is buried at the Villers Station Cemetery, Villers-au-Bois. He is shown wearing the insignia of the Royal Berkshire Regiment together with the RFC wings on his left breast.

CSM George Henry Inman receiving his Distinguished Conduct Medal from King George V at Battle Hospital, Reading. CSM Inman joined the Regiment in 1904. He went to France on the outbreak of war with the 1st Battalion, and won the DCM at the Battle of Loos in 1915. His brother, William John Inman, also of the regiment, won the DCM whilst serving with the 2nd Battalion British West Indies Regiment in Egypt. They are the only brothers of the regiment to achieve this double distinction.

The Clemetson brothers from Milman Road, Reading. Both were in A Company, 1sr/4th Battalion. Frederick (left) and his brother Will were mobilised with their battalion in 1914 and went to France. Fred was killed on 25 August 1915, together with four other soldiers from Reading when a 4.2in shell landed in the brickfields where they were billeted. They had just returned from bathing. Fred is buried in Hebuterne Military Cemetery. His brother Will survived the war. They are seen here with the pre-war 1906 pattern leather equipment, which polishes well, but is no good in wet and muddy conditions.

Colonel Walton, commanding officer of the 8th (Service) Battalion. On the outbreak of war he was on leave in England from his appointment in India. He was tasked to raise and train the 8th Battalion which he did with great efficiency. Veterans from the battalion remember his training methods were hard, but served them well later. He went into action with his battalion on 25 September 1915, at the Battle of Loos. His battalion received praise in Haig's dispatches. He himself was gassed at that time and after convalescenting was posted to Aden.

Sgt Owen Attewell, 9th Battalion, shown here in 1915, was not a career soldier but a pre-war school teacher, being the master of Welford and Wickham school, which was located a few miles from Newbury. He started his war service in Welford, as a special constable but enlisted on 14 August 1915, into the Royal Berkshire Regiment. His potential for leadership was quickly spotted and he was promoted to full corporal. By October the same year he was promoted to sergeant. He remained with the battalion for a year receiving a commission in 1916 into the 4th Battalion Royal Fusiliers. By 1917 he had risen to the rank of Major and over the year that followed won a Military Cross and Bar. The finale of his army career was when he rode at the head of the 4th Fusiliers into Cologne. After the war he returned to Welford and his profession of teaching. In 1921 he took up the position of Master of Hungerford Council Elementary School.

The pride of the 'Sixth'. This trio of soldiers contain the youngest and oldest soldiers of the 6th (Service) Battalion Royal Berkshire Regiment in 1915. Seated are Ptes 'Hobby' Lark and 'Lottie' Collins. The young boy is drummer Crayford. All three survived the war.

Drum Major Davey, 1st/4th Battalion, who had served in the Berkshire Volunteers for thirty-two years. He volunteered for foreign service on the outbreak of war, but was blocked by Colonel Serocold, who transferred him to the newly raised 2nd/4th Battalion. On being transferred, the Corps of Drums played him to the station. Pictured with him are his three sons, two of whom served in the signalling section of the 4th Battalion and the third in the RAMC.

Lt William Poulton-Palmer, 1st/4th Battalion went to Oxford University in 1908 where he represented the university at hockey for three years. His real passion was rugby and he played for England seventeen times. In 1914 he captained England when they beat Wales, Ireland, Scotland and France. Whilst at Oxford he was a keen member of the OTC and in 1912 joined the 4th Battalion Royal Berkshire Regiment at Reading. On the outbreak of war he immediately volunteered for foreign service and went to France on 30 March 1915. On the night of 4/5 May 1915, whilst in command of a working party, he was hit by a rifle bullet and died instantaneously He was the first officer of this battalion to fall and is buried at the Hyde Park Corner (Berks extension) Cemetery, France.

Sgt Day, Royal Berkshire Regiment, in the First World War. The second button down on Sgt Day's tunic is black in colour. This unofficial, but accepted, practice shows that he was in mourning for someone close.

Above: Ptes Thomas and William Millard from Davis Street, Hurst, Berkshire. Both of these brothers were pre war regular soldiers. During the war William served in the 1st, 2nd and 5th Battalions. Both brothers were wounded in action and discharged in 1916 as unfit.

Right: Cpl Welch VC was a pre-war regular soldier and a regimental athlete of note. He particularly excelled at cross-country running. At the start of the First World War he came back to England with the 2nd Battalion from India, later transferring to the 1st Battalion. It was with the 1st Battalion in 1917 that he won the Victoria Cross at Oppy Wood. During his time on the Western Front he was wounded five times, and fought at Neuve Chapelle, Fromelles, Loos and Ovillers, with the 2nd Battalion, and Delville Wood, Beaumont Hamel and Oppy with the 1st. He died in 1978 at the age of eighty-eight. His medals are on display at the Regimental Museum at Salisbury.

Lt Turner VC, (3rd Bn attached) 1st Battalion, was the son of Major Charles Turner, a long service Royal Berkshire Officer from Thatcham, Berkshire. He joined the 1st Battalion in France in June 1915, being wounded soon after. On 28 September 1915, during the attack on Fosse 8, at the Battle of Loos, he led a party of battalion bombers down a trench known as 'Slag Alley'. Together with four men he drove the Germans back about 150 yards, being severely wounded in the process. He died from his wounds on 1 October 1915, and is buried at Chocques Military Cemetery, France. His brother, Lt-Col V.B. Turner, also won a VC in the Second World War with the Rifle Brigade, and they were also related to General Sir Redvers Buller VC.

Capt Harold Ackroyd VC, medical officer of the 6th (Service) Battalion. Although Capt Ackroyd was not a Royal Berkshire-badged soldier, he considered himself to be one. He only ever served with the 6th Battalion, sailing to France with them in July 1915. He took part in most of the battalion actions, saving the lives of many men who would otherwise have perished. He was awarded a Military Cross for his work in Delville Wood in 1916. He survived the opening day of the third Battle of Ypres on 31 July 1917, but was killed eleven days later in Jargon trench, Glencorse Wood. He is buried at Birr Cross Roads, Cemetery, Zillebeke, near Ypres. His wife Mabel received his Victoria Cross from the King at Buckingham Palace on 26 September 1917. He received the VC for his actions on 31 July 1917. He died without knowing about the award.

CQMS Fred Woodhouse, 6th Battalion, enlisted at Lambeth and went to France on 25 July 1915. He is seen here in full fighting order next to a chalk-carved China Dragon, depicting the regimental cap badge. This carving is now in the Regimental Museum at Salisbury. He was killed in action on 2 October 1916, at the Schwaben Redoubt, and is buried at Blighty Valley Cemetery, Authuile Wood, Aveluy.

Sgt Maj Alder 1st/4th Battalion, a pre-war regular soldier who had joined the Regiment in 1908. He was awarded the DCM for leading a patrol that captured twenty prisoners in Italy during the First World War. He was also awarded an Italian Silver Medal for the same action. He received his DCM from General the Earl of Cavan, the C. in C. of British Forces in Italy, at Granezza. In the photograph the 'Royal Berks' shoulder flash is clear, but the number '4' has been removed by the censor. He later became the RSM. After the war he remained with the regiment serving in Iraq, Persia and India. On the outbreak of the Second World War he rejoined and became the first RSM of the newly raised 6th Battalion.

CSM Plank DCM & Bar, MM MID, 1st Battalion. He joined the 3rd Battalion as a Special Reservist on 19 March 1908, and in November 1914 joined the 1st Battalion in France. His first DCM was won in 1917, at Oppy Wood, the same action in which Cpl Welch won his VC. After the war he went with the 1st Battalion to Mesopotamia, and remained with this Battalion until his retirement in 1935. On retirement he became a drill hall caretaker for the 10th Hackney Battalion (later 5th Battalion Royal Berkshire's). He died in 1939.

Private Mulford, 6th (Service) Battalion 1918. Seen here in full fighting order with Respirator on his chest. On his left lower sleeve he is wearing a good conduct stripe indicating three years' service under which he displays a wound stripe. In the First World War he was wounded twice. He remained in the army after the war serving in India, with the 1st Battalion, rising to the rank of Sergeant Major. After retirement he settled in Abingdon. On the outbreak of the Second World War joined the 11th Battalion of the Berkshire Home Guard, becoming a machine gun instructor.

Opposite below: L/Cpl F. Pockett, 1st Battalion Royal Berkshire Regiment, was the battalion champion boxer. He was also the battalion representative at 'putting the shot', a member of the tug-of-war team, and winner of the light heavyweight championship, army and air force in India, 1931.

Above: Private Frank Gray was born in Oxford in 1880 and was educated at Rugby School. He became a solicitor and held a number of legal appointments until he resigned in 1916 to join the army. Declining promotion, he served throughout in the ranks, joining the 8th Battalion of the Royal Berkshire Regiment in June 1917. He served in 6 Platoon B Company remaining with the battalion until the end of the war. After the war Frank Gray led a colourful life. He worked with labourers in order to study their conditions and toured the Oxfordshire workhouses as a tramp. He is shown in the photograph in one of his disguises. In 1926, by way of a change, he crossed Africa from west to east in fifty-eight days driving a 7hp Jowett car, one of a pair called 'Wait' and 'See'. He served on the Oxfordshire County Council, was a JP and was also the Member of Parliament for Oxford City from 1922–1924. His publications included: *Confessions of a Private*; *Confessions of a Candidate*; *The Tramp* (1931) and numerous political pamphlets. He died in 1935.

Left: Major F.S. Boshell, DSO MC, enlisted in the regiment in 1887 and served in the ranks until 1908, when he was commissioned Lieutenant and quartermaster. His grandfather and father had served in the regiment, so he naturally followed them. He himself was followed by his son Frank. During the First World War he came into his own as the QM of the 1st Battalion on the Western Front. He never let the battalion down ensuring the re-supply of ammunition and food reached the front-line troops even under enemy fire. After his retirement, he became the secretary to the Princess Christian's convalescent home at Woking. He died in 1937.

Above left: Corporal L. Bates, 2nd Battalion, winner of the Corporals Challenge cup, Aldershot Command 1930. His equipment is still as worn during the First World War. On his left forearm he displays his weapons qualifications badges, Marksman (crossed rifles) and LG (light machine gun).

Above Right: Brigadier Dennis Walter Furlong DSO, OBE, MC, Royal Berkshire Regiment. He was the most senior officer of the regiment to lose his life in the Second World War. In September 1940, he was a brigade commander in Yorkshire, and in whose brigade the 1st Battalion formed a part. He was killed in an accidental explosion caused by a 'mushroom mine'. His intelligence officer Lt M.D.P. Magill, also of the Regiment and a pre-war England cricketer, died in the same accident. Brigadier Furlong is buried in Kilham and Lt Magill was cremated at Darlington where he is commemorated.

Opposite below: Major 'Frankie' Boshell seen here receiving a well-deserved DSO from Lord Louis Mountbatten at Johore Bahru, Singapore, in 1946. He had been a company commander with the 1st Battalion both at the Battle of Kohima and in subsequent operations on the Mandalay Plain, in Burma, where he led B Company in three and D Company in two decisive actions, advancing over 200 miles in the process. As well as his DSO Major Boshell was also mentioned in dispatches. Major Boshell's father had served in the Regiment with distinction also being awarded the DSO in the First World War. In 1963, Frank Boshell became the third commanding officer of the 1st Battalion Duke of Edinburgh's Royal Regiment (Berkshire and Wiltshire).

A rare picture of Major Bruce Charles Neville Dawson MC, Royal Berkshire Regiment, attached to the 4th Parachute Brigade, as brigade major, to Brigadier Hackett. Major Dawson went to France in 1939, where he was wounded and received an award of the Military Cross whilst serving with the 1st Battalion. He was later attached to the airborne forces and dropped at Arnhem where he was killed in action by a sniper on 20 September 1944, the day after this photograph was taken. In the photograph he is shown with a sling on his left arm having been wounded in a counter-attack. He is buried in Arnhem Oosterbek War Cemetery. He was also the brother-in-law of Colonel Rupert Mayne, the grandson of Captain Mayne who commanded the 3rd Light Cavalry at Maiwand in 1880.

Major Harry Kitney joined the Regiment in 1919 and gained promotion rapidly; he was a sergeant by 1922 and a company sergeant major by 1927. He was one of the regiment's finest shots. In 1936 he became RSM of the 1st Battalion and, in 1940, its quartermaster. Col Bickford later remembered, 'We fetched up together at Dunkirk and spent two or three days mustering the remnants of 6 Brigade near the beaches; he was on that occasion a tower of strength and worked unceasingly giving no thought to crossing the Channel (unlike so many others who found they had urgent business in England) and it was then that I first became aware of his sterling qualities'.

He remained with the battalion throughout the war, serving in the Burma campaign including the action at Kohima. He remained in the regiment after the war serving at home and in the Middle East. He retired in 1956, having been awarded the MBE.

Lt John Ellis, 1st Battalion, was killed in a terrorist action in Eritrea. He was gazetted to the regiment on 20 October 1948, and joined A Company in March 1949. He quickly made his mark as a sportsman, and was particularly active in anti-Shifta operations. On 7 March, leading his patrol, he left Adi Ugri and followed up a Shifta gang, starting seven hours behind them. Contact was made with the gang after a hard march at Amadir, where he was mortally wounded. His men carried him back five miles to transport where his last words to them were about a wounded soldier from his unit. He was buried at Asmara.

Two stalwarts of the 4th/6th Battalion, the regiment's territorial battalion, c.1964. From left to right: CSMs Pete Reader and Tommy Baynham, winners of the NRA Volongdis cup for the Bren gun pair. Both good shots, they represented the battalion in shooting competitions over many years. CSM Reader was previously a national serviceman with the Dorset Regiment. On demob, he joined the 4th/6th remaining with them for the remainder of his TA service, including time with the 1st Bn Wessex Regiment (TA), retiring in 1976. WO Baynham followed his father into the regiment as a regular soldier, his father having lost both legs in action in the First World War. On demob from the regulars he joined the 4th/6th and later helped form the Wessex Regiment (TA). On retirement, he emigrated to Australia. (Volongdis is short for 'Volunteer Long Distance Cycling Cup'.)

Sgt Alan Ault, 1st Battalion, shakes the hand of the Colonel of the Regiment, General Sir Miles Dempsey, after winning the BAOR, Machine Gun Cup at Goslar, West Germany. *c.*1955. Looking on is Lt Tremellen, the machine gun platoon commander. Lt Tremellen's father had served in the regiment losing an arm in the First World War. The divisional sign worn on Sgt Ault's arm is the 'Charging Bull' of the 11th Armoured Division. The battalion's brigade was the 91st Lorried Infantry Brigade.

C/Sgt Kingswell, Military Medal (Left) and Maj. Frederick Myatt, Military Cross, both of the 1st Battalion Royal Berkshire Regiment, in Goslar, Germany, *c.*1955. Major Myatt enlisted in the Grenadier Guards in 1935, and by the age of twenty-two had attained the rank of Lance Sergeant, one of the youngest in the Brigade of Guards. He obtained a commission in the Royal Berkshire Regiment in 1940, and later that year was seconded to the Gold Coast Regiment with whom he won his Military Cross in Burma. Later, he returned to the regiment and served with them in BAOR, Malta and Cyprus. On retirement he set up the museum and library at the School of Infantry at Warminster, Wiltshire, and published a total of thirteen books on military matters. He also produced a basic dictionary in the Hausa language in which he was fluent.

Signaller Les Devine, a national serviceman of the 1st Battalion, on patrol during the EOKA campaign in Cyprus 1956–59. He is man-packing a radio-set and carrying a Sterling sub-machine gun, wearing the cold weather clothing issued for operations in this theatre of operations. Most of the Battalion were national servicemen at this time, but a hard core of regular's maintained continuity.

Three Regimental Sergeant Majors of the Royal Berkshire Regiment, Brock Barracks, Reading c.1955. From left to right: RSM Green (Depot RSM), RSM Baston DCM (1st Bn) and RSM Allen (4th/6th Bn). RSM Baston was awarded his DCM for action with the BEF in 1940. After the war he served in Eritrea with the 1st Battalion, on one occasion engaging the Shifta rebels at pistol point.

The Royal Berkshire Regiment was very much a family regiment with generation after generation following each other into the regiment. Pictured in front of the Maiwand Memorial in Forbury Gardens, Reading, in around 1962, are three generations of the Kew Family. On the left is Captain D. Kew, MC and Bar, DCM, MM, who enlisted into the Regiment on 1905. He was awarded the DCM and MM for gallantry whist serving in the 2nd/4th Battalion on the Western Front during the First World War. He was later commissioned and went on to win the MC and Bar with the Bedfordshire Regiment. He continued to serve with the regiment after the war. His son, Colour Sergeant C. Kew (centre), joined the Regiment in 1947 after war service in the Royal Artillery and continued serving until the amalgamation with the Wiltshire Regiment in 1959. Colour Sergeant Kew's son, Pte V. Kew, joined the newly formed Duke of Edinburgh's Royal Regiment (Berkshire and Wiltshire) and was followed by his younger brother.

RSM L. Hodges, the last RSM of the 1st Battalion, pictured here shortly after the amalgamation with the Wiltshire Regiment in 1959, when he became the first RSM of the new Duke of Edinburgh's Royal Regiment (Berkshire and Wiltshire). He was the son of a former member of the regiment and joined as a boy soldier in 1934. He joined the 1st Battalion in Shorncliffe where he soon made his mark as a boxer and good shot. In 1937 he was posted to the 2nd Battalion in India where he won the Battalion Open Welter-weight Boxing Championship. He spent most of the Second World War instructing in India and England. After the war he served both with the regular and territorial battalions of the regiment finally taking over as the RSM of the 1st Battalion in Cyprus in 1958.

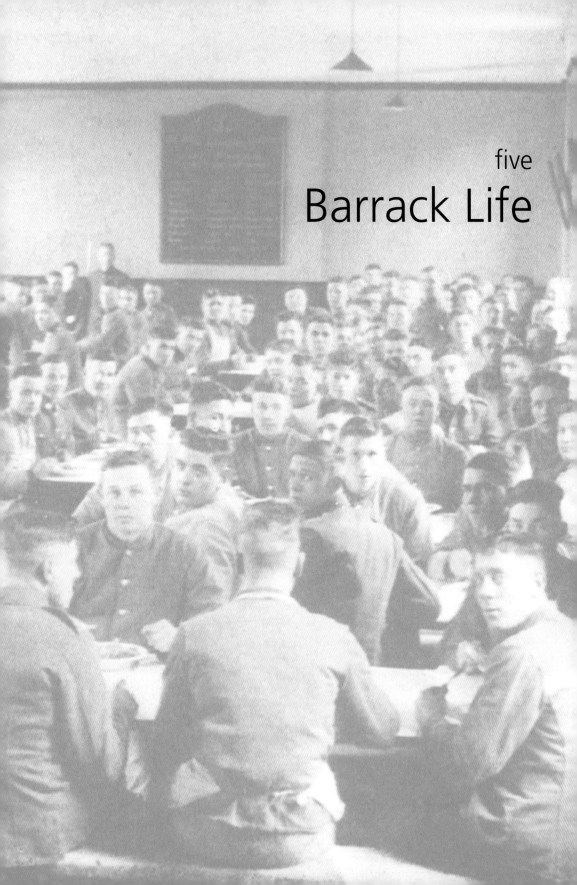

five

Barrack Life

Above: A sight familiar to generations of Royal Berkshire soldiers, the regimental depot, Brock Barracks, Oxford Road, Reading. It was named after General Sir Isaac Brock, a 49th of Foot officer who rose to prominence during the campaign in Canada in 1812. This barracks started being used as the regiment's depot in 1878 when the depot companies of the 49th and 66th Regiments amalgamated. It remained the regiment's home up until 1959. The keep is now a listed building, and used by local community groups in Reading. The remainder of the barracks is still in use by the territorial army.

The Regimental Cenotaph, Brock Barracks, Reading. Here it stands next to the keep, but has since been moved to another part of the barracks, and still forms the focal point for regimental remembrance. It was designed by Sir Edwin Lutyens RA, and closely followed in smaller proportions the pattern of the National Cenotaph in Whitehall. It is carved from Portland stone, and stands 17ft, 9in height. It commemorates the 353 officers and 6,375 men of the regiment who fell in the First World War 1914–1918, and the ninety-three officers and 974 men who fell in the Second World War. Contained inside the cenotaph is the roll of honour naming all the men.

The armoury, Brock Barracks, Reading, c.1932. A well-polished part of the barracks that housed all the weapons required by the recruits in training.

Opposite below: A view of the interior of Brock Barracks c.1952, from the top of the keep. It shows the square with several barrack blocks on the far side. The names of these blocks have changed over the years, but the two main blocks were originally named Tofrek and Anson respectively. To the left is the officer's mess. All the buildings in view are still in use today by the territorial army and cadet units.

On 26 June 1937, the Regiment hosted an 'At Home' day at Brock Barracks, Reading. Over a seven hour period they had 17,600 visitors through the gate. The displays were manned by the recruits and they are shown here re-enacting an incident on the North West Frontier of India, a country that some of the recruits would visit in the near future.

The depot dining hall in Brock Barracks, Reading, c.1933. Recruits in training taking their mid-day meal. At this time regimental cooks fed the regiment having received their training at the Army School of Cookery at Aldershot. The Army Catering Corps was not formed until 1941.

Six likely lads who had just been recruited into the regiment *c.*1931. They are pictured behind the main barrack block in Brock Barracks, Reading, well away from public gaze. Shortly after this photograph they would be processed through the system prior to joining one of the two Regular Battalions. At this time there were 100 recruits being trained with the majority going to the 2nd Battalion in India. During 1931 a *Daily Mail* reporter visited the Barracks and likened what he found to be more of a public school than a barracks.

Those same six recruits are part of this recruit squad putting the finishing touches to their arms drill on the square at Brock Barracks, Reading, in 1931. The parade square is still in use today by the territorial army, but the tennis courts seen to the rear has become a housing estate.

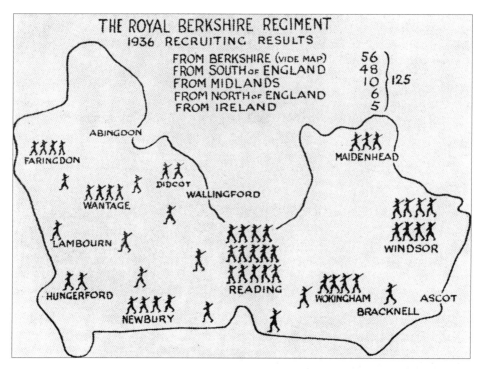

THE ROYAL BERKSHIRE REGIMENT
1936 RECRUITING RESULTS

FROM BERKSHIRE (VIDE MAP)	56
FROM SOUTH OF ENGLAND	48
FROM MIDLANDS	10
FROM NORTH OF ENGLAND	6
FROM IRELAND	5

125

ABINGDON
FARINGDON
MAIDENHEAD
DIDCOT
WALLINGFORD
WANTAGE
LAMBOURN
WINDSOR
HUNGERFORD
READING
NEWBURY
WOKINGHAM
BRACKNELL
ASCOT

A snap shot of the recruiting situation in 1936. The regiment did its utmost to recruit from the county. At that time Faringdon and Wantage had the highest proportion of recruits compared to their population. Between the wars the regiment recruited heavily from London and Birmingham.

The 'September' squad of new recruits, c.1925, prepare to go out for a day's trip, from Brock Barrack, Reading. These recruits would not be allowed to be seen by the general public until the instructors were happy that their turnout and bearing were up to the regimental standard.

Regimental Concert Party, 1st Battalion, Fyzabad, India, c.1930. Anybody with a bit of talent, including family members, were always encouraged to take part.

A kit inspection sometime between the wars for a Royal Berkshire battalion 'In the Field'. The kit is laid out in a pre-determined order so the inspecting officer can see at a glance if anything is missing. These soldiers have fixed their 'Bedplates' to the front of the bed blocks. The bed plate would normally be fixed above the soldier's bed in barracks. It is a brass plate with the soldier's name, rank and number stamped into the metal, together with the regimental badge. It is said that when a soldier died in service the bedplate would double as a coffin plate.

Sgt and Mrs Ashley, with their daughter, together with the officers' mess staff, 1st Battalion in Bareilly, India, c.1920. Sgt Ashley would have been responsible for the efficient running of the mess and maintaining regimental standards. He was assisted by his wife and a considerable number of Indian servants. The Indian servants would remain with the battalion throughout its stay and would remain in post for the incoming regiment.

1st Battalion, Fyzabad, India, c.1929. The social side of life for the families was not neglected, as is illustrated in this photograph of a sergeants' mess tennis party. All the children were involved. The mess walls are adorned with photographs and regimental paintings. The mess silver, mainly sporting trophies, is displayed at the rear.

The 1st Battalion, polo team, Fyzabad, India, 1929. Winners of the Perry Challenge cup, having beaten the 60th Rifles. From left to right; Lt Drake-Brockman, Capt. K.P. Smith, Lt D. Sinclair, Lt H. du P. Finch. Whilst in barracks in India and Malta, the regiment fielded a reasonable team, sometimes beating cavalry teams in the process. Capt Smith had war service with the 2nd/4th Battalion on the Western Front and later served in Russia and Nigeria. On the outbreak of the Second World War, he commanded the 6th Battalion, and later commanded the 1st Malta Brigade during the siege. He went on to command 185 Brigade during the Normandy landings. Lt H. du P. Finch. on the outbreak of the Second World War, went on to take over the 6th Battalion from Lt-Col K.P. Smith, and later took command of the 2nd Battalion in Burma, where he was awarded the DSO.

The 2nd Battalion on the march into Crownhill Barracks, Plymouth, c.1923. Many of the new recruits were sent from Brock Barracks to the 'Home' Battalion for continuation training, where route marches played a crucial part in their training to become proficient infantrymen. Led by Major Tremellen (who lost his arm during the First World War) the men are seen here marching to attention. Major Tremellen later became a Lieutenant Colonel and served during the Second World War. His son later joined the Regiment.

2nd Battalion, 14 November 1936. The 'Four-in-hand' team, arriving at the Union Club, Port Said, from the officers' mess, Moascar, as a result of a wager. Running time was six hours with two teams. The team pictured here consisted of Lt-Col Leslie MC, Capt. Dillon MC (RASC), Lt Macdowell, Lt Nelson.

2nd Battalion, Regimental Race, South Berkshire point-to-point, Sonning, 17 April, 1929. A large crowd watches the start. From left to right; Polly (Lt Warren), Toby (Lt Wilder), Flame VI (Lt Millard), Wexford (Lt MacDowel), Bedale (Capt. Burney), Delilah II (Lt Arthy), Smallwood (Major Issac). Officers stationed at Brock Barracks between the wars were regular participants in the local hunts and point to points.

The 1st Battalion on parade in period costume on the occasion of the Aldershot Tattoo in 1936. On this occasion the battalion was the major unit involved. This high profile annual event always attracted large crowds. In 1936 the battalion also appeared as Roman soldiers.

The 4th/6th Battalion Football team, Winners of the Territorial Army, Southern Command and Salisbury Plain Challenge Cups 1956/57. This team was the most successful ever fielded by the Regiment. Back row: CSM Bishop, Pte Chapman, Pte Buckle, L/Cpl Wheeler, Pte Passey, Pte Harding, Sgt Jones, RSM Hodges. Front row: Pte Borton, Pte Lambert, Lt-Col Metcalf (Commanding Officer) Pte Gutteridge (Captain), -?-, -?-, -?-. (inset) Cpl Mortimer, Pte Werrell. Most of the players were national servicemen who had completed their full-time two years' service in the Regiment and were now engaged in their obligatory follow-up period of service in the Territorial Army.

The Royal Berkshire company from Bulford marching past the Mayor of Newbury, Major Bradshaw MC, after General Sir Miles Dempsey, the Colonel of the Regiment had received the freedom of the town on 23 July 1947. The Mayor was originally in the Scots Guards and took part in the siege of Sidney Street, London, when a pitched battle was fought against anarchists who had murdered three police officers. He became the youngest RSM in the British Army. When commissioned, he chose the Royal Berkshire as his regiment and it was with them that he won his MC in 1918. The right guide for the company is Sgt Maj. George Whitewick.

All barracks were little towns which were served by civilian staff of many years' standing. This is the last regimental Christmas party held in the gymnasium, Brock Barracks, 1958. Lt Col A.L. Taffs, DSO OBE, together with three of the N.A.A.F.I. Staff, all of whom would have been known to the many thousands of recruits who passed through the barracks. The ladies are Mrs Sylvia Dibley, Miss June Carter and Mrs Marjory Jones.

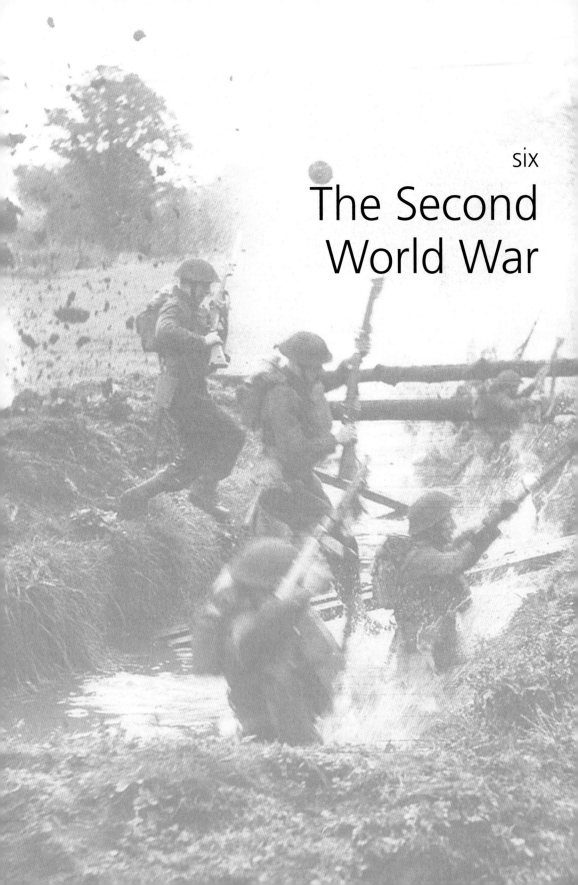

six

The Second World War

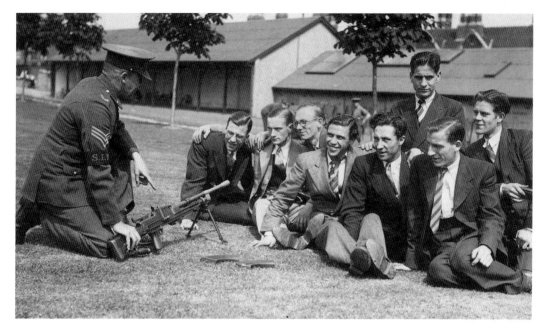

Above: Sgt Young, an instructor at Brock Barracks, Reading, giving a weapons lesson in 1939 on the Bren gun to recalled reservists of the Royal Berkshire Regiment. Most of these men would have had experience of weapon handling, although the Bren gun may have been unfamiliar to them as it had only recently been introduced into the British Army.

Below: King George VI visits Brock Barracks, Reading, in 1939 shortly after the outbreak of war. The King is talking to Major Hunt whilst the training corporal oversees bayonet training. The recruit with the rifle is no doubt being instructed to 'put some beef behind it'.

The officers, 1st Battalion, Blackdown Camp, Aldershot, 1939. The battalion was in the 6th Brigade, of the 2nd Division in which, by coincidence, the 1st Battalion was serving on the outbreak of the First World War. Back Row from left to right: Lt Crichton, 2nd/Lt Shaw, 2nd Lt Sedgwick, Lt Findlater, 2nd/Lt Waleun, 2nd/Lt Panter, 2nd/Lt Daniel, Lt Thomas (KIA 16.5.40), Lt Dawson (KIA 20.9.44, Awarded MC). Centre Row, from left to right: Lt Mongomerie (RAMC), Capt L.A.B. Robinson, 2nd/Lt Magill, 2nd Lt Buckham, Lt Riddell, Capt. Bickford (Commanded at Kohima), Lt Davis, 2nd/Lt Allen (KIA 15.5.40), Lt Hall (KIA 25.5.40), Revd Roberts (Chaplin). Front Row, from left to right: Maj. Carr, Maj. Rew, Maj. Elliot, Capt. Niven, Lt-Col Dempsey MC, General Sir F. Ready (Colonel of the Regiment), Maj. Hanney, Capt. Watney, Capt. Harvey (KIA 2.3.44), Capt. Alpin, Capt. Groombridge (Quartermaster).

Lt-Col Dempsey took the battalion to France, shortly after he was promoted to command a brigade. Thereafter, his promotion was rapid. Under General Montgomery he was chosen to command the 2nd (British) Army, up to and including D-Day, until the end of the war in Europe.

Men of the 1st Battalion mount guard outside their headquarters at Herbaum, near Orchies, on the Franco-Belgium border in 1939. With events of the First World War still in mind gas masks, seen here, were carried at all times. This was the period known as the 'Phoney War' when, to help alleviate possible boredom, pre-war standards of drill and personal turn-out were vigorously maintained. Note the hand-operated siren in the foreground.

Soldiers of the Royal Berkshire Regiment carrying out a task that has bedevilled generations of infantrymen, in this case road-building fatigues in France, acting as labourers for the Royal Engineers, during the 'Phoney War' in 1939/40. They are using home-made rammers to lay the foundation of a cobblestone road. Just visible in the background is a Bren gun mounted for possible enemy air action.

Anti tank gunners, of the 1st Battalion, in a pill box on the Franco-Belgium Border in 1940, one of three pill boxes that they manned. Here they prepare a 2 pounder for action. These soldiers are still in the pre-war service dress with puttees which were replaced by the battledress just before the German 'Blitzkrieg' and the retreat to Dunkirk.

Right: The 1st Battalion man trenches on the Gort Line in France in 1940, during the phoney war. This photograph is somewhat posed, the reality proved to be a lot untidier. This showpiece series of breastworks were known as 'The Lambeth Walk'.

Below: Soldiers of the 1st Battalion practice counter attack manoeuvres, shortly after their arrival on the Franco/Belgium Border. Training was intensified during this time, with live firing exercises on the newly issued anti-tank rifle, and the 2in mortar. This training enabled the battalion to sharpen up the reservists.

Soldiers of the Royal Berkshires in a Universal Carrier, proudly show off their war 'booty' to the citizens of Reading during a 'Wings Week' fund-raising campaign in 1941. Substantial numbers from the regiment transferred to Nos 3 and 4 (Army) Commandos for the raid on the Lofoten Islands, Norway, in March 1941 and later, the Dieppe raid in 1943.

Opposite above: In early 1940, whilst the 1st and 4th Battalions were recovering from the events at Dunkirk, the 2nd Battalion were still in India. Here, we see the Battalion on a swimming parade. This battalion remained in Lucknow, Bombay and Madras from 1939 to 1942. In 1943 they moved to the Arakan where their war started in earnest.

Opposite below: Officers of the 5th (Hackney) Battalion at Bournemouth just prior to the D-Day landing at Normandy, where they were tasked to land on Juno Beach as a beach group battalion for the Canadians, landing at Bernieres sur Mer on 6 June 1944. Back row, from left to right: Lt Phillips, Lt Lucas, Lt Wyeth, Lt Beale, Lt Spackman, Lt Holly, Lt Hodges, Lt Pyke, Lt Holme, Lt Tarrant, Lt Josey. Centre Row, from left to right: Capt. Pardoe, Capt. Bedford (KIA 22.9.44), Maj. Vines (KIA 18.4.45), Capt. Chapman, Capt. Prior, Lt Marsh, Capt. Martin, Lt L' Etang (MO), Capt. Woodroffe. Front Row, left to right: Capt. (QM) Child, Maj. Brown, Maj. Smith (KIA 8.10.44), Lt-Col Taffs, Maj. Gen. Collins (Colonel of the Regiment), Maj. Board, Maj. Todd Capt. Jenkins.

Lt Tarrant was cross posted after the landing to the 5th Battalion Wiltshire Regiment where he won the Military Cross and was wounded. He is the father of Chris Tarrant, the television celebrity.

The 6th Battalion, Coleraine, Northern Ireland, *c.*1941 These photographs were taken from a film produced for British Movietone News. This was shown in the news bulletins in all cinemas in Great Britain and at the Chicago Exhibition, USA, and images reproduced in the American magazine *Life.* They were also dropped over Germany by the RAF for propaganda purposes. This photographs shows the troops on the assault course.

6th Battalion, Northern Ireland, *c.*1941. A section in full fighting order, advancing at the double behind smoke. A high priority was placed on fitness throughout this training.

Soldiers of the 6th Battalion advance through a barbed wire entanglement, the soldier in the rear is using a Thompson sub-machine gun, to provide covering fire. Although not yet at war, America was, nevertheless, sending weapons and other war-like supplies to Great Britain, including the Thompson sub-machine.

River crossing in full kit during the 'Blitz Course'. Here a member of the 10th Battalion heaves his comrade out of the river. For this part of the exercise their weapons are secured to the small packs on their backs.

Soldiers of the 10th Battalion, undertaking a 'Blitz Course' to harden them up, and to prepare them for the rigours of battle. Here, men in slit trenches are supported by Bren Carriers. The vehicles are named after regimental battle honours; the one nearest the camera carries the name 'Egmont-op-Zee'.

As training progressed, so did the use of live ammunition. Seen here are soldiers of the 10th Battalion assaulting a position, supported by Bren Gun Carriers. The Battalion left England well trained, as their subsequent performance in Italy later showed.

His Majesty the King, on a visit to the 10th Battalion, in training. Here he is being shown the equipment being carried by a sergeant, who is armed with a Thompson sub-machine gun, otherwise known as a 'Tommy gun'. In the background soldiers of the battalion are formed up ready for an attack.

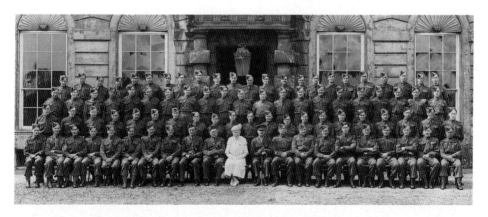

Badminton Detachment, No.1 Independent Company, Royal Berkshire Regiment, 1944. They were part of 'Goldfinch' Detachment, the codeword for Badminton, the Residence of Queen Mary. In December 1942, the 30th Battalion was stationed in Corsham, Wiltshire. In January 1943, two platoons of D Company were dispatched to carry out this duty under the command of Captain Mant MC. In April the same year they were due to change over when Queen Mary made a special request that they remain. As a result the Royal Berkshire detachment stayed until the cessation of hostilities.

Young soldiers of the Royal Berkshire Regiment, Army Cadet Force, at camp in
Windsor Great Park *c*.1943. With wartime rationing in force these cadets had the chance
of three square meals a day whilst at camp, and this was enough to ensure their locust-
like appetites were satisfied.

The 5th Battalion on Juno Beach on the evening of 6 June 1944. German prisoners are
marched off to awaiting landing craft to take them to England and the prisoner of war
camps. Capt. Peter Prior, the battalion intelligence officer, controls the second group
of prisoners by the DUKW. Behind that vehicle is the 8th Beach Group headquarters.
The White Ensign outside the hotel is the Royal Naval beach master's headquarters.
The seawall has been blasted and levelled to make a wheeled exit from the beach. The
complete battalion was ashore in three hours, and earned 'Normandy Landing' as a battle
honour for the regiment.

Medics of the 8th Beach Group, and 5th Battalion, under the supervision of the
5th Royal Berkshire Medical Sergeant, attend to the wounded on Juno Beach
who, at this stage, were mainly Canadian but with some British and a few Germans
also. Although the pill box behind has been silenced, the close proximity of the
enemy is evident by the trench-digging activity. Members of the beach group were
identifiable by the painted white bands around their steel helmets.

Men of the 5th Battalion are seen here digging in within 300 yards of the river
Rhine in preparation for the assault crossing on 23 March 1945. The battalion had
been specially selected by the 2nd Army commander, General Miles Dempsey, to
perform a similar role to that undertaken in the Normandy Landings. They earned
for the regiment the battle honour 'Rhine Crossing'.

A Wasp flame thrower, Essen, Germany, June 1945, is manned by soldiers of the 5th Battalion. Private Smith is driving with Sergeant Wiltshire on the right.

Whilst the 5th Battalion prepared for and then landed in Normandy, the 10th were fighting their way up through Sicily and Italy. Here, a fully equipped rifle section of the 10th Battalion make their way up to the front line in Italy in 1943. The use of mules to carry the heavier loads was common to all battalions in this theatre. Troops in the Italian theatre acquired, unfairly, the sobriquet 'D-Day Dodgers'.

Above: Soldiers of the 10th Battalion make their way along a muddy mountain track north of Roccamfina, Italy 1943. The battalion spent a number of days in this village prior to the battle of Mont Camino. They returned to the village afterwards for rest. This group is led by a sergeant, and none are looking at the camera, indicating they are concentrating on the conditions and task ahead.

Right: Soldiers of 'Sawyers Battalion', the wartime code name for the 10th Battalion, after action on Mont Camino, Italy, November 1943. The battalion fought for four days on this mountain, sometimes hand to hand. Six German attacks were repulsed in the first twelve hours. The condition of the soldiers tells the story.

Both the regular battalions of the regiment fought in Burma as part of the 14th Army, which later became known as the 'Forgotten Army'. Here we see the 2nd Battalion on the outskirts of Mandalay, Burma, taking cover behind ancient carriages whilst waiting for the order to advance. Once inside Mandalay, the battalion were tasked to take the formidable obstacles of 'Mandalay Hill' and 'Fort Dufferin'.

The start of the attack on Mandalay Hill, March 1945, by soldiers of the 2nd Battalion. Large packs and bush hats have been left behind, and steel helmets are worn with bayonets fixed. After the hill was taken all that remained was the central walled area of 'Fort Dufferin'.

Soldiers of the 2nd Battalion, moving through the Bazaar area of Mandalay, March 1945. The approach march to Mandalay was sixteen miles with full large pack, weapons and ammunition. Although hampered by snipers, the battalion made fast progress.

Soldiers of the 2nd Battalion advance into the village of Madaya, en route to Mandalay. They entered the unoccupied village on 7 March 1945, but soon came under attack from the Japanese. They remained in the village for two days, repelling the Japanese, before resuming the advance on Mandalay.

Some of B Company, 2nd Battalion, before crossing the Chindwin River, November 1944. Among those pictured are Lt Ridley (KIA 27.12.44), Sgts Heywood (DOW 14.3.45, awarded DCM) and Barratt, (KIA 30.1.45), Cpls Stowe and Barratt, L/ Cpls Horton, Brown (KIA 10.3.45), Heath (DOW 7.1.45), Sion and Dodd, Privates Murray, Biggington, Baker, Bunn (awarded Military Medal), Elwell, Dodd (KIA 10.3.45, awarded Military Medal & MID), Moore, Lacey, Fuller, Thompson, Stewart, Armsby (KIA 8.1.45), Rainsford, Allwright (KIA 6.3.45), Legett (KIA 26.1.45) and Birch.

A group of soldiers of the 2nd Battalion in Burma at the end of the campaign with their 'Spoils of War'.

The battlefield of Kohima after the battle, 1944. The 1st Battalion was the first battalion of the 2nd Division to relieve the besieged Royal West Kents. Once in position the battalion continued to do battle with the fanatical Japanese for a further five weeks. The commanding officer, Lt-Col Bickford, later remembered, 'The first thing that most upset us was the incredible filth and stench, the garrison had not been able to bury corpses or dig latrines or refuse pits due to snipers, shelling and mortaring.' The battalion continued to fight and operate in conditions that soldiers of the First World War would recognise.

The Kohima Memorial Cross erected by the 1st Battalion, in memory of their comrades who fell in the Battle of Kohima, April–July 1944. The original wooden marker was erected on 'Summer House Hill', Kohima. The Battalion lost two officers and fifty-six men killed, and fifteen officers and 239 men wounded. The battle honour 'Kohima' was granted to the regiment.

Headquarters Company 30th Battalion. As members of 'T' Force, they joined the 21st Army Group in February 1945 in Holland. The previous year, the battalion had been given five days to mobilise in preparation to take part in the re-occupation of Guernsey as part of Force 135. This was cancelled shortly afterwards, and they were diverted to Holland.

C Company, 30th Battalion, at the Liberation of Rotterdam on 8 May 1945. This was unopposed as the Germans capitulated the day before. This photograph was taken from the back of a lorry by C Company's interpreter Mr Hoek. The dispatch rider is Private Jackman.

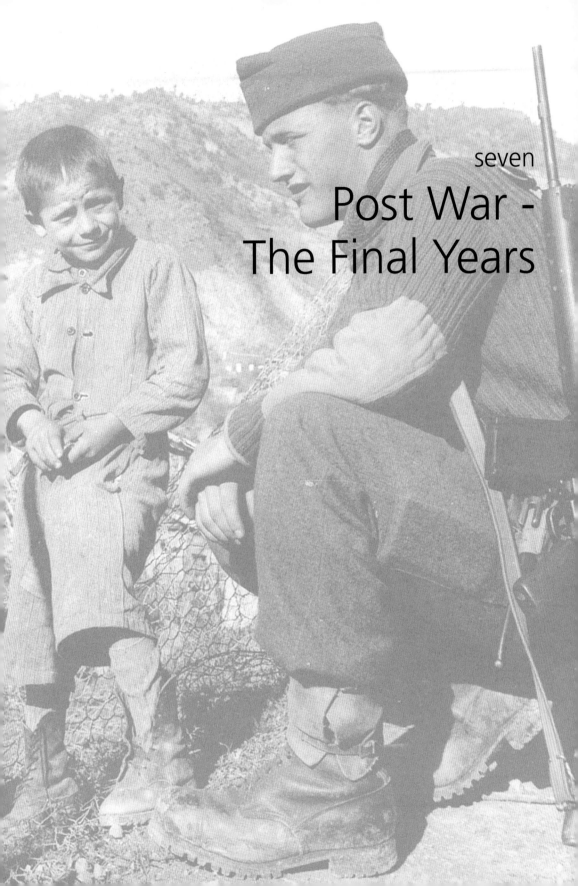

seven

Post War - The Final Years

The Anti-Tank Platoon, Support Company, 2nd Battalion, Mingaladon, Burma, 1947. The battalion had sailed from England for Palestine in 1934 and later moved on to Egypt. By the time war broke out they were in India. They were the last British battalion to leave Burma in 1948. Centre of this picture is one of the Anti-Tank Platoon section commanders, Cpl 'Lofty' Allcock. He served a full twenty-two years, retiring from the Duke of Edinburgh's Royal Regiment in 1969.

The band of the 2nd Battalion in Burma 1947. The band was disbanded in 1942 and re-formed on 15 July 1946. The first parade for the newly constituted band was a farewell parade for the 4th Ghurkhas who were leaving Burma. Thereafter they practised hard to try and reach their pre-war standards.

The 2nd Battalion arrived in Eritrea from Burma, via Egypt, in 1948, as part of the response to the activities of the Shifta rebels. It was in Eritrea that what remained of the 1st Battalion joined them, and there the two Battalions were amalgamated as a result of the post-war army reductions. In addition to operating against the rebels the battalion made great strides to gain its pre-war smartness. Here, the newly amalgamated battalion marches past carrying the colours of both the 1st and 2nd battalions on 5 March 1949.

Soldiers of the 1st Battalion look on at a group of captured Shifta rebels, Eritrea, 1949. The battalion was allocated the Serai Division, located in the south-west corner of the country, and bordering on Ethiopia. They acted in support of the Eritrean Police Field Force. At this stage many of the young soldiers in the battalion were national servicemen.

1st Battalion, Eritrea 1949, seen here questioning captured Shifta rebels. A lot of the battalion activity centred on the area of Adi Ugri, where the resident rifle company found it necessary to react almost daily in response to rebel contact.

1st Battalion on operations against the Shifta Rebels, Eritrea, 1949. Soldiers from the battalion are seen here loading mules for an operation where the wild and mountainous country would exclude the use of vehicles.

Soldiers from the 1st Battalion man a road block in Eritrea, 1949. Although sometimes boring, roadblocks were nevertheless extremely important. It hindered the Shifta in their movements and therefore kept them off balance. Here, soldiers from the 1st Battalion check out a local truck.

Newcomers arrive at Asmara station, in this case two RAF men with their kit bags. The 'Litorino' rail bus has just made its way up from the port of Massawa, a journey sometimes at risk from Shifta attack. As a consequence armed escorts were usually provided, frequently by soldiers from the regiment.

Members of 4 Platoon, B Company, 1st Battalion, at the jungle training camp at Agordat. The Regimental Journal records that one section of this platoon was 'put to flight' during this training exercise by soldier ants that were reputed to be two inches long!

The dangers of anti-terrorist operations are only too clear when troops engage the enemy in short but sharp actions. Soldiers of the 1st Battalion reverse arms at the funeral of Lt Ellis, who died from his wounds after an engagement at Amadir against the Shiftas on 7 March 1951.

Above: The Signal Platoon, 1st Battalion, Suez Canal Zone, *c.*1952. The battalion consisted of a high number of National Servicemen at this time. The battalion arrived in Egypt from Cyprus in 1951 and remained in the Canal Zone until 1953. The General Service Medal and Clasp, for service in the Canal Zone, was only authorized in 2003 after a long campaign. Included in this photograph are Sgt Roy Fuller, Cpls Brenan, Cross, Kew, Hayward, Ptes Conner, Gillian, Coo and Rockwell.

Right: The G.O.C-in-C Southern Command, Lt-Gen. Sir Ouvery Roberts K.B.E. C.B. D.S.O., M.A. watches a demonstration of a medium machine gun operated by Sgt L. Chapman of Maidenhead, and Private P. Smith, during a visit to the Annual Camp of the 4th/6th Battalion, at Mytchett, in around 1950.

The 1st Battalion, disembark from HMT *Empire Clyde* at Liverpool on 24 April 1953 after returning from Egypt. They are being greeted by the colonel of the regiment, General Sir Miles Dempsey. The troops pictured are from the Support Company, included are Maj. Boshell DSO, Maj. Pardoe and Sgt Strong.

The 1st Battalion march through Hanover, West Germany, with drums beating, bayonets fixed and Colours flying on the occasion of the Queen's birthday parade, 9 June 1955. The Colour party consists of Lt Tremellen, Lt Redding, RSM Baston DCM, followed by the company commanders Maj. Myatt MC and Maj. Blascheck MC.

The successful machine gun team, from the 1st Battalion, Goslar. They were winners of the BAOR Cup 1955, against very stiff competition. In the centre is colonel of the regiment General Sir Miles Dempsey. Sitting, from left to right: Sgt Alan Ault (Platoon Sgt), Lt Tremellen (Platoon Commander), General Sir Miles Dempsey, Lt Col. Speers (commanding officer), -?-.

Ski team of the 1st Battalion, in the Harz Mountains, West Germany. This was a necessary skill required by the battalion at this time as the western side of the border needed constant patrolling. The battalion worked in conjunction with the 'Bundesgrenzschutz', which had just been raised by the West German authorities to patrol the border between East and West Germany. The battalion remained in BAOR until May 1956.

Corps of Drums 4th/6th Battalion (T.A.), 1960. Rear, from left to right: L/Cpl A.M. Fisher, Dmr R.M. Wallace, Dmr P. Keenagh, Dmr S.J. Eltham, Dmr J. Davis. Centre, from left to right: L/Cpl S. Judd, Dmr A.N. Davey, Dmr B.G.Duckett, Dmr R Boardman, Dmr S.J. Ray, Dmr J. Strudley, Dmr L. Wardle. Front row, from left to right: D/Major A.G. Jones, RSM J. Price, Lt- Col. L.J.L. Hill M.C (CO), Capt. P.T. Dunn (adjutant) and Sgt E.A. Courtney. Lt-Col. Hill won his Military Cross with the 2nd Battalion in Burma. RSM Price was later commissioned and became the Regimental Museum curator, Capt Dunn went on to serve in the Duke of Edinburgh's Royal Regiment, and became a Queen's Messenger.

In 1960 the 4th/6th Battalion travelled to Millom in Cumbria, for its annual camp. This was a year at the height of the Cold War and the battalion was in the home defence role. Here Major General Cubbon, GOC 43rd (Wessex) Division, talks to one of the battalion's rescue teams during training. Lt-Col. Hill (in battle dress) is shown to the left of the GOC.

In 1959 the 4th/6th Battalion paraded in the Forbury Gardens, Reading, to celebrate the centenary of the formation of the Berkshire Rifle Volunteers, the Battalion's forbears. Here, they are seen marching past the Berkshire Territorial Association Chairman, Air Marshal Sir Robert Saundby. The Forbury gardens have been the focus for many of the regiment's events, as it is here that the 'Maiwand Lion' proudly stands, in commemoration to those of the 66th (Berkshire) Regiment who fell, in 1880 at the Battle of Maiwand in Afghanistan.

Alderman Clifford Atwell, the Mayor of Wallingford, handles the new Self Loading Rifle, then just coming into service. Lt-Col. Hill MC looks on anxiously. The occasion was a 4th/6th Battalion recruiting campaign held throughout Berkshire in 1960.

Territorial soldiers of the 4th/6th Battalion, disembark at Cherbourg from HMS *Finisterre*, for Exercise 'Autumn Crocus', in October 1960. Major C.H. Willing acted as commanding officer for the exercise.

Exercise 'Autumn Crocus', France, *c.*1960. Warrant officers and Sgts of the 4th/6th Battalion, 'liaise' with their French counterparts. Regimental members are Sgt Wailes, C/Sgt Timms, CSM Baynham, CSM Reader, and CSM Wyatt. Most of the Territorial Army annual exercises took place in England, so the opportunity to operate in France was welcomed. The red 'Brandywine flash' worn behind the China Dragon Cap badge is proudly displayed.

Gunners of the 648 Heavy Anti-aircraft, (Royal Berkshire, Hackney) Regiment, Royal Artillery, seen hear firing the guns during annual camp in Towyn, North Wales *c*.1953. During this year they also won the Brigade Challenge cup for all-round efficiency.

Gunners of the 648 Heavy Anti-aircraft (The Royal Berkshire, Hackney) Regiment, Royal Artillery (T.A.) being inspected during their annual camp at Towyn, North Wales. This regiment started life as the 10th London Regiment, later to become the 5th Battalion Royal Berkshire Regiment. After the war they were re-designated as Royal Artillery. They still wore the Royal Berkshire Regimental Cap badge, The China Dragon, but they also wore the shoulder titles of the Royal Artillery. The regiment was finally disbanded in 1955.

In response to the Suez Crisis, the 1st Battalion, was flown from the United Kingdom to Malta in August 1956, where the troops trained and acclimatised at the seashore camp of Bahr-I-Caghar, where this photo was taken. The only part of the battalion to go to Suez was the anti-tank platoon. When events stabilized in Suez the battalion went to Cyprus to face the EOKA terrorist campaign. They were to remain in Cyprus for three years. Most of these soldiers are national servicemen, but some of the regular soldiers identified in the front row are Sgt Way, CSM Pearson, Sgt Duncan (with beard), CSM Leadbetter, Sgts Middlecote, Peters, Willis and Kelly.

The anti-tank platoon of the 1st Battalion are seen here firing their 17-pounder anti-tank guns out to sea. The regiment had been sent to Cyprus as a result of the Suez crisis. There they were reinforced with reservists and prepared for the operation. In the event only the anti-tank platoon deployed, providing an anti-tank capability for 40 Royal Marine Commando, under the command of Lt Robin Wilson.

With Port Said burning in the background, 1st Battalion Royal Berkshire anti-tank gun detachments disembark from their landing craft on 6 November 1956 as part of the Anglo-French assault. The vehicle displaying the recognition letter 'H' is a turret-less Stuart light tank which carries one of the battalion's anti-tank detachments.

An anti-tank gun section of the 1st Battalion is seen here in a suburb of Port Said shortly after landing. The anti-tank gun on the left of the photograph is the American 106mm 'recoilless rifle' which was rushed into service for the operation. The other weapons shown are all of Second World War vintage. With the shortage of enemy armour to engage, the CO of 40 Commando tasked the detachment to remove a troublesome sniper. With a chance to fire their new '106' in anger the detachment hauled the gun on to the roof of the Egyptian army barracks and fired at the offending sniper. Not only did they remove the sniper but also the building he was operating from. From left to right: Pte 'Lofty' Mason, from Newbury, -?-, Pte Boylen, -?-, Pte Davis, Pte Hill.

Soldiers of 'C' Company, 1st Battalion, employing donkeys to carry equipment over the difficult and rugged terrain during the operations against EOKA terrorists in the Troodos Mountains, 1957. The three leading men are, from left to right, Pte Haywood, Pte Coates, Pte Woodley.

Although the battalion was tasked for internal security in Cyprus, military skills still had to be maintained. A sudden contact with a terrorist group in a rural setting would need an instance response and weapon handling skills, therefore, were as vital here as anywhere. Pte Morris of A Company is shown practising firing the Bren gun from the hip in a close quarter situation. The date is March 1957.

The laying of ambush positions at night in the Troodos mountain range was a tactic widely used. Good discipline and nerve were required and while many of the soldiers considered that the results did not always justify the efforts, the tactic did, nevertheless, have the effect of restricting terrorist movement. Soldiers from 2 Platoon, A Company, are seen here returning to their platoon location after a fruitless night in April 1957.

A Soldier of A Company, 1st Battalion, in the village of Pelendria, Cyprus, March 1957, talking to two young boys. The hearts and minds approach often produced more results than the heavy-handed approach. The soldier is carrying the newly-issued FN self-loading rifle which was gradually replacing the No. 4 .303 Lee Enfield bolt action rifle.

A Company's lines at Primasole Camp in 1957. The camp was about three miles to the west of Nicosia and virtually on the end of Nicosia airport's runway. It was the battalion's base camp from late November 1956 until its departure in the spring of 1959. Living conditions were rudimentary, but the soldiers soon learned to adapt and make themselves comfortable. Only a limited amount of time was spent in these base camps. Most of the time the soldiers were either on stand-by or on operations. Here we see the 'Char Wallahs' dispensing the inevitable 'char and wad'. The morale boosting Char Wallah was an indispensable part of battalion life. Usually from Pakistan, their family businesses would go back many generations to pre-partition days in India. Many a battalion move or operation would first be announced through the Char Wallah's grape-vine.

During the first half of its tour in Cyprus, many operations were undertaken in the Troodos mountain range lasting any from a few days to twelve weeks. The operations usually started at first light with a 'cordon and search' of a village, or indeed many villages. Code names, such as 'Black Mac' 'Brown Jack' 'Green Dragon' and 'Lucky Mac' were used to name only a few. Here soldiers of the 1st battalion search the village of Pelendria, March 1957. Pte Morris, manning a Bren gun, keeps his eye on the local men.

Soldiers of 2 Platoon, A Company, gather before an operation in January 1957. They are wearing supposedly 'wind proof' smocks but these did little to keep out the wind in the cold Troodos winter. The majority of these soldiers were national servicemen.

Soldiers of 2 Platoon, A Company, rest during a rural operation in February 1957. Constant movement in difficult country was sufficient to keep the battalion at a high level of fitness during the campaign, although new arrivals always needed hardening up to cope with the mountainous terrain.

A Section of 'B' Company, 1st Battalion, on patrol in a back street of Nicosia, Cyprus, during the EOKA campaign. The patrol leader is L/Cpl Peter Stacey, from Newbury, armed with the new Sterling sub-machine gun. This patrol is only a few yards away from Ledra Street, otherwise known as 'Murder Mile'. L/Cpl Stacey served for many years eventually retiring as a major (QM).

For the second half of the Cyprus tour the battalion changed from an island wide-role to responsibility for Nicosia and its environs. Here we see a 'Cat Patrol', wearing plimsolls and cap comforters, patrolling the backstreets of Nicosia at night. The lead soldier is carrying a Belgium FN rifle. With later modifications, this weapon entered service as the self-loading rifle (SLR).

Soldiers of support company set up an emergency road block in Nicosia, Cyprus, c.1958 during the EOKA campaign. These snap road checks were used to great effect to disrupt the movements of the terrorists.

Signaller Les Devine of the 1st Battalion, Signal Platoon, during Operation 'Whisky Mac'. Signallers were vital in providing communications in the mountainous areas where the use of vehicles meant travelling along slow and tortuous tracks. He is armed with the new FN self-loading rifle.

Tofrek Platoon, Brock Barracks, Reading, 1952. this is just a representative group to illustrate the large number of Royal Berkshire Regiment national servicemen who went through the barracks. This platoon was named after the Battle Honour 'Tofrek' that resulted in the regiment being designated a 'Royal Regiment' by Queen Victoria in 1885. From left to right, back row: Ptes Barton, Ellaway, McCarthy, Gray, Lovelock, Clifford, Goodman, Brewer. From left to right, centre row: Ptes Pettifer, Heath, Bell, Crossway, Annetts, Hulbert, Davis, Cox, Kinch, Gee, Hickman, Lines. From left to right, front row: Ptes Fisher, Lobb, Cpl Budden, Capt Savill, Sgt Hollingsworth, 2nd Lt Nankivell, Ptes Hyde, Clark. Pte McCarthy later became a long-standing chairman of the Reading branch of the Old Comrades Association.

A passing-out parade of young national service soldiers at Brock Barracks, Reading. The keep is visible in the background. The platoon passing out is 'Maiwand' Platoon of 1956, and it was an opportunity for friends and family to see the change ten week's training had made. After a short spell of leave, the soldiers would join the battalion. The majority of those in this platoon would join the 1st Battalion on operations against the EOKA terrorists in Cyprus. Maj. Ward leads the parade followed by Lt Coniford and Sgt Oxley. The first three recruits are, from left to right, Ptes Ford Devine, Mason.

The Band and Drums of the 1st Battalion, lead the battalion for the last time on the farewell parade marching past the Queen Victoria statue in Friar Street, outside the town hall in Reading on 14 May 1959. Similar farewell parades took place throughout the county of Berkshire during this time, after which the regiment prepared to amalgamate with the Wiltshire Regiment.

The last Guest Night for the officers of the 1st Bn Royal Berkshire Regiment, Brock Barracks, Reading, 22 May 1959. Back Row, from left to right; Lt Morris, Lt Jones, Lt Greenway, 2nd/Lt Devlin, 2nd/Lt Kerwood, Lt Mathews, 2nd/Lt Ravenhill, 2nd Lt Goodhart. Middle row, from left to right; Lt Nash, Lt Reid, Lt Macmillan, Capt. (QM) Green, Capt. Ward, Capt. Hobbs, Capt. Tremellen, Capt. Williams, Capt. (QM) Webb, Lt Vernon-Powell, Lt Aylin. Front row, from left to right: Maj. Higgins (RAPC), Maj. Hunter, Maj. Brown, Maj. Myatt, Lt-Col Bromhead, Brigadier Hogg, Lt-Col Hill, Maj. Forster, Maj. Youde, Maj. Farmer, Maj. Stone.

Above: The Royal Berkshire Regiment troop the regimental colour of the 1st Battalion for the last time on 20 May 1959 at Brock Barracks, Oxford Road, Reading. The colour is carried by 2nd Lt D.A. Jones and the escorts to the colour are Sgts Cross, Leader and Aldridge.

Below: The final parade on 22 May 1959, with Windsor Castle's Round Tower providing the backdrop. The colours are draped over piled drums in a low key ceremony. Canon Pike officiates before the colours are taken to the Royal apartments for the final laying up.

The final chapter in the story of the regular element of the Royal Berkshire Regiment, the laying up of the colours at Windsor Castle on 22 May 1959. Both colours have just been handed over for safe keeping where they were placed on the grand staircase next to the disbanded Southern Irish Regiments.

The colours (right) in their final resting place at Windsor Castle, where they remain today. The regiment amalgamated with the Wiltshire Regiment on 9 June 1959, when the battle honours, traditions and history of the Royal Berkshire Regiment (Princess Charlotte of Wales's) were carried forward into the Duke of Edinburgh's Royal Regiment (Berkshire and Wiltshire).

Other local titles published by Tempus

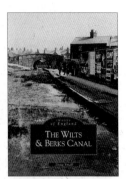

Wilts and Berks Canal

DOUG SMALL

The Wilts & Berks was conceived late in the canal boom and was always doomed to failure. Ironically, its busiest period was in the 1830s when the canal transported the building materials for the Great Western Railway – which then killed off its trade. Towns grew up around and on top of it, but it remained in good condition. It is now slowly being reclaimed from the mud, weeds, old cars and other rubbish that choke its path.

07524 1619 7

Kennet and Avon Canal

CLIVE & HELEN HACKFORD

Construction on the Kennet and Avon canal began in 1794, a safe route from London to Bristol avoiding the hazardous English Channel. Attempts to close the canal in the 1940s failed and the 1950s saw the formation of what was to become the Kennet & Avon Canal Trust, who rebuilt the neglected waterway. One of the most spectacular of England's waterways, the Kennet & Avon has become the biggest success story of canal restoration.

07524 2129 8

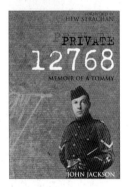

Private 1278 Memoir of a Tommy

JOHN JACKSON

This is the remarkable memoir of John Jackson, who in 1926 wrote up the diary he kept throughout the war and his vivid recollections of the conflict. Jackson was an ordinary Private who saw the worst of the conflict, but whose belief in the just fight of the British Army and his respect for his superiors never wavered. His narrative captures the devotion and courage of the soldiers of the day. It has remained unpublished until now.

07524 3184 6

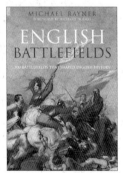

Illustrated Encyclopaedia of English Battlefields

MICHAEL RAYNER

In this ground-breaking volume, covering over 500 battlefields, Michael Rayner strips away later features and land use on the many battle sites of England and uses contemporary accounts, archaeology and military history to reconstruct the events and give clear, concise accounts of the battles which shaped England.

07524 2978 7

If you are interested in purchasing other books published by Tempus, or in case you have difficulty finding any Tempus books in your local bookshop, you can also place orders directly through our website

www.tempus-publishing.com